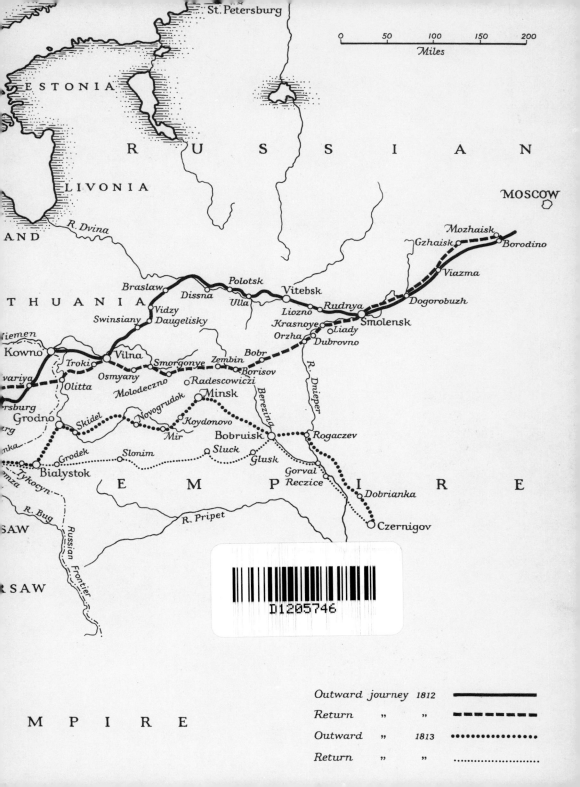

WITH NAPOLEON IN RUSSIA
1812

WITH NAPOLEON
IN RUSSIA

1812

The diary of Lt H. A. Vossler
a soldier of the Grand Army
1812–1813
translated by Walter Wallich

Lithographs by
Christian-Wilhelm von Faber du Faur

LONDON
The Folio Society
1969

PRINTED IN GREAT BRITAIN
Printed by Richard Clay (The Chaucer Press) Ltd, Bungay
Set in 'Monotype' Baskerville 11 point leaded 2 points
Lithographs printed by Stellar Press Ltd, Barnet
Bound by W & J Mackay & Co Ltd, Chatham

Contents

Illustrations

Introduction

'Instead of the four hundred thousand companions who had fought so many successful battles with them, who had swept so masterfully into Russia, they saw emerging from the white, ice-bound wilderness only a thousand infantrymen and troopers under arms, nine cannon and twenty thousand stragglers dressed in rags, with bowed heads, dull eyes, ashen, cadaverous faces and long, ice-stiffened beards . . . this was the Grand Army.' The words are those of Count Philippe-Paul de Ségur, Napoleon's aide-de-camp during the Russian campaign, describing the return of the Grand Army's stricken remnants across the Niemen in December 1812. And the concluding words of his history of the campaign sum up the fascination it holds for us to this day: 'The noise of such a fall will echo down the ages, in which great misfortunes bring immortality as surely as great glories.' The very dimensions of the catastrophe make it a subject for never-ending speculation and the stuff of which the world's great literature and poetry are made.

Whatever the causes of the disaster, lack of foresight and preparation can hardly be numbered among them. Napoleon was certainly well aware of the hazards of the enterprise and the type of campaign he would probably have to fight. His advisers were almost unanimous in warning against it. As for his enemy's strategy, Tsar Alexander had made it crystal clear to him, through the French Ambassador in St Petersburg, that he proposed to avoid battles that might destroy his armies, and to let the vastness of Russia and the rigours of its soil and climate do his work for him. Napoleon, moreover, had been closely studying the history of Charles XII of Sweden, whose military genius came to grief against these formidable obstacles in the previous century.

Nor does Napoleon seem initially to have intended to make

the mistake of penetrating deep into enemy territory, except cautiously and by stages. The Austrian Foreign Minister, Count Metternich, recounts the following conversation he had with Napoleon in Dresden on the eve of the campaign. The Emperor told him: 'My undertaking is one of those where the solution is to be found in patience. Victory will go to the most patient. I shall open the campaign by crossing the Niemen and it will be concluded at Smolensk or Minsk. There I shall stop and fortify those two points. At Vilna, where the main headquarters will spend the next winter, I shall busy myself with organizing Lithuania which is impatient to be freed from the yoke of Russia. I shall wait and see which of us tires first—I of feeding my army at Russia's expense, or Alexander of maintaining my army at the expense of his country. Perhaps I myself shall spend the most inclement months of the winter in Paris.' Metternich asked Napoleon what he would do in the event of the Tsar not making peace despite the occupation of Lithuania, to which the Emperor replied: 'In that case I shall advance next year to the centre of the Empire, and I shall be patient in 1813 as I shall have been patient in 1812: I have already told you, the affair is a question of time.' According to the Swiss war historian Henri de Jomini, who was in the Emperor's entourage, Napoleon was still airing the same ideas even at Vilna, though by then he was already in two minds about his future conduct of the campaign.

If Napoleon, for reasons that are no clearer to us today than they were to his contemporaries, abandoned a strategy which required patience, but at least did not court disaster, Tsar Alexander carried out his by accident rather than design. Whatever his own intentions, his generals, in the initial stages of the campaign, were only too eager to give battle. If they failed to do so it was not for want of trying, but because they were constantly being outmanoeuvred by the French. No sooner had they selected a position from which to fight than they found themselves outflanked or outnumbered and forced to resume their retreat. It was because of General Barclay de Tolly's failure to halt Napoleon's progress into the depths of the country—the very strategy the Tsar had planned—that Alexander had to replace him as commander-in-chief with General Kutusov who, paradoxically, shared the Tsar's views but fought the campaign's only major battle—at Borodino—reluctantly and because it was unavoidable.

As for Napoleon's preparations for the campaign, they were elaborate, far-sighted and impressive. Planning started eighteen months before it was launched. From January 1811 onward troops, supplies and funds were gathered and readied in every part of Napoleon's Empire, from Spain to the Baltic and from the Atlantic to East Prussia. Great care was taken over the preparation of maps of Russia. Masses of stores were assembled in depots all over Germany. Even forged Russian banknotes were printed with which to purchase supplies if, as seemed likely, the Army found itself unable to live off the land. (There is no evidence, incidentally, that this money was ever used.) Perhaps the best example of meticulous planning was provided by Marshal Davout's First Corps, stationed in Northern Germany. Its seventy thousand men were provided with supplies for twenty-five days. Each company included artificers of every description, from masons to bakers and from tailors to gunsmiths. They carried with them everything they could possibly need, plainly prepared to find the country to which they were going devoid of even the most elementary necessities. The Corps was like a colony on the move—every emergency had been foreseen and the means of meeting it prepared. There were even handmills for grinding corn.

Admittedly Davout's Corps was by far the best disciplined and equipped of the Army, but preparations generally were on a similarly elaborate scale. As far as the Niemen the plan was to use supplies stored at Mainz, Magdeburg and Danzig. Seventeen battlions of transport, with 5,000 to 6,000 carts and bullock wagons, were designed to move two months' provisions for 200,000 men. The carts required 8,000 to 10,000 drivers, 18,000 to 20,000 horses and oxen, in addition to the 100,000 odd horses of the artillery and cavalry. Ship- and bridge-building material required another 2,000 horses for its transportation. Napoleon hoped to feed this vast mass of animals by deferring the opening of the campaign until the appearance of grazing.

It was the very vastness of these preparations, perhaps, which proved the ultimate cause of the disaster. Others certainly contributed to it: In the first place, Napoleon himself was past his prime, ailing, and except for occasional flashes of brilliance, a mere shadow of his former self. Then there was the composition of his huge army, more than half of it drawn from some twenty nations few of which had much stomach for the fight. Furthermore, Tsar Alexander displayed far greater steadfastness and strength of purpose in adversity than the best judges of his character had given him credit for. The Russian generals, though no match for Napoleon and his Marshals at their best, were experienced and competent enough to preserve their armies from destruction. Above all, these armies, fighting on their own soil, for their homes and their native land, maintained a standard of discipline and morale which Napoleon's motley host could never hope to equal.

But in the last resort, it was the very scope of the operation that ultimately proved unmanageable. 400,000 soldiers, 120,000 animals—not counting the herds of cattle each corps drove along with it—6,000 wagons, 12,000 guns: it was a problem in logistics with which the techniques of the early nineteenth century were simply not equipped to cope. In the words of Napoleon's fellow-countryman, Montaigne: 'Great and distant enterprises perish from the very magnitude of the preparations made to ensure their success.'

The South German State of Württemberg gained enormously in territory and wealth from the wars of the French Revolution and those of Napoleon, thanks largely to the enterprise and shrewd diplomacy of Duke Frederick II, who reigned from 1797 till 1816 and raised the status of his country to that of a kingdom. He started by fighting the French and got beaten. He changed sides and was handsomely rewarded for it by Napoleon. Finally, with Napoleon's fortunes on the wane, he switched his allegiance once more, ending the long succession of wars and campaigns still on the winning side. In the process he increased his country's territory by a third and its population by half a million. Though he was linked by close family ties to Russia—Tsar Alexander was his nephew and two of his brothers held senior commands in the Russian Army—he did not allow this to stand in the way of his diplomacy. No doubt it helped him to make his peace with Russia and Prussia in 1813 and to benefit, to the tune of five million guilders, from French war reparations.

As a ruler, Frederick was an autocrat, constantly at odds with his country's rudimentary parliament. On declaring himself King he abrogated the constitution. He lived in considerable style and maintained an establishment somewhat out of proportion with his country's wealth and standing. He was not greatly loved by his people, but on balance probably did Württemberg a great deal more good than harm.

Among those of his subjects who took part in the revolutionary and Napoleonic wars there were several who kept diaries or wrote books about them, and one, Faber du Faur, whose illustrations of the Russian campaign became famous. The diary of Heinrich August Vossler has not previously been published.

Vossler was born in 1791 in the small Württemberg town of Tuttlingen, the third child of Johann Vossler, steward of the local church domaines. Johann Vossler was the son of a teacher and started his professional life as a clerk. By hard work and a talent for organization he achieved the quite eminent position of an administrator of Church property, which as a rule was open only to men of substance. At the age of fifty he established his social standing in the community by marrying the daughter of the town's foremost apothecary, a girl thirty years his junior. Contemporary records indicate that he was a contentious man who repeatedly fell foul of the civil administration. He lived with his family in a handsome house which today is the site of the local law courts.

It is, perhaps, from his father the clerk that Heinrich Vossler learned the copperplate handwriting in which his diary of the wars of 1812 and 1813 is written. His father's gift for organization also emerges from the methodical way in which the diary is constructed. Each section begins with a historical summary of events, followed by a description of the countryside and people, and concludes with an account of the author's own experiences and adventures. Apart from one or two minor lapses he is extremely accurate about dates and place names. Considering the conditions in which he was writing this was a remarkable feat.

From his comments he emerges as an educated man with good powers of observation, a keen and enthusiastic eye for scenery and architecture, a liking for good and civilized living and a sense of history and politics. He seems also to have had a sense of humour. His attitudes reflect pretty faithfully those of the times. A Protestant by religion he adopts a sceptical attitude towards the Catholic Church, but he is sufficiently open-minded to admire the religious rites of other denominations and, on occasion, to be moved by them. He echoes the conventional prejudices of the South German about his fellow countrymen in the North. His views about the Poles and the Russians do not differ in any way from those of most Germans, whether of his day or ours. Indeed, these parts of his diary could equally well have been written by a German officer serving on the Eastern front in the Second World War. It is perhaps worth noting, however, that in Vossler's case they seem to stem less from conventional prejudice than from personal observation. Far from having any preconceived notions about conditions in Poland, he suspected that the North Germans' lurid and depressing accounts of them were inspired by pure malice.

If Vossler's descriptions of the countryside through which he passed at speed tend to read like a third-rate guidebook, his accounts of conditions on the march and of life in Poland and Russia are as vivid as they are shrewd. What to the modern reader is probably the most glaring omission is the lack of a personal relationship with the troops he commanded. Apart from an occasional reference to his personal servants—usually in connection with his mounts and equipment—or to a senior N.C.O., they feature mainly as an irritating impediment to rapid travel. The alacrity with which he and his fellow officers, both on the retreat from Russia and on the homeward march

B

from captivity, seem to have left them to fend for themselves appears rather shocking to our modern way of thinking. But in judging his relations with them we must bear in mind the very different ideas on man management prevailing in Vossler's day and the far greater social gulf between officers and men. That his attitude towards his charges was not entirely callous is shown by the account of his vain efforts to marshal remnants of the Württemberg contingent during the retreat from Moscow.

Vossler concludes his diary with a brief but poignant summary of the state—both physical and financial—to which two years of active service had reduced him. But though at the time of writing his future must have seemed bleak it provided him, in fact, with an active, useful and not unrewarding existence. As the recipient of the Knight's Cross of the Military Order of Merit he was entitled to call himself *von* Vossler, as if he had been of noble birth, and as a war invalid he was entitled to an appointment in the civil service. He seems to have availed himself of this privilege and to have had a reasonably distinguished career in the Württemberg finance ministry. When he died in 1848, at the comparatively early age of fifty-six, he was head of the finance department in the Württemberg town of Herrenberg. The appointment, in the service of the State, was not unlike that which his father had held in the service of the Church. We know that he was married and had at least one son, who emigrated to the United States.

My thanks are due to the Stuttgart State Archives and to Rektor H. Streng, Curator of Archives of the town of Tuttlingen, for their help in tracing the family background and career of Heinrich Vossler.

WALTER WALLICH

Author's Preface

My parents had intended me to study, but before I was old enough to enrol at a university the King* had issued a decree that in future only the sons of State servants, who were privileged to wear his coat-of-arms on their buttons, should be allowed to study without special permission. My father was a servant of the Church and lacked this privilege. So I had to seek royal consent. The year was 1809 and predictably, in the prevailing circumstances,† permission was refused. So I became a clerk. But I disliked the job and was, in any case, convinced that I would sooner or later be called to the Colours. So I finally persuaded my mother (my father having died in the meantime) to allow me to enrol in the Army as a volunteer cadet. I entered upon my military career in June 1809 with the depot company of the Footguards and took part in several small skirmishes against the Vorarlberg insurgents. The following year I was transferred, at my own request, to the Royal regiment of Light Horse as an ensign and promoted four weeks later, in June 1810, to a second lieutenancy in another cavalry regiment—the 'Duke Louis' Chasseurs. I was stationed, first in Zwiefalten, then in Ettlingen and finally in Riedlingen.

We had now enjoyed two whole years of peace—a state of

---

* Frederick II of Württemberg (reigned 1797–1816).

† A royal decree on conscription for the armed forces, dated August 1809, listed eight categories of Württemberg citizens who could pursue university studies without special permission. The children of lay servants of the Church, such as Vossler's father, were not among them. Vossler senior, moreover, had repeatedly come into conflict professionally with the State authorities. The incorporation, in 1806, of Church lands for which, in the parish of Tuttlingen, he was responsible, with those of the State may well have led to further friction. In the circumstances his son was unlikely to be granted the special dispensation he needed, even though Vossler senior was by then no longer living.

affairs as irksome to the veterans as to the newcomers. Promotion on garrison duties was slow, and many had got into debt or other troubles that made a change of scene, and especially a new war, seem desirable. I personally had been preserved from debt by a disagreeable but salutary circumstance,* so this was not my problem. But I was bored with garrison life and all its attendant trivialities, and by conversation revolving exclusively around horses, women and wine. Principally, however, it was the hope of rapid promotion and a thirst for adventure which made me long for a war as fervently as any of my comrades.

* Although Vossler's father was a man of considerable standing in the community and the family was well off, there is some evidence that after his death their financial affairs fell into disarray. It may have been this experience which restrained Vossler from squandering his money.

PART ONE

I

I T was early in February 1812 that we received the long
awaited order recalling all troops from leave. Life suddenly
became very busy, but merry withal. I took advantage of a few
days' furlough to bid my mother and family in Tuttlingen
farewell.

On 17th February 1812, a beautiful, spring-like day, we
moved out of our quarters at Ettlingen, Riedlingen and Blau-
beuren and began our march through lower Württemberg.
Through Zwiefalten, my former garrison, our road took us by
way of Stuttgart to Eglesheim near Ludwigsburg, where we arrived on 20th February. The following day we passed in review
there before the Inspector-general of Cavalry. General von Dillen, and later before the King, but neither the one nor the other
took much notice of our regiment or its colonel, whose standing
was not of the best.

By 23rd February we were on the march once more, reaching
the outskirts of Heilbronn on the 24th. This was the assembly
area of the Württemberg army corps, and a river-side meadow
near the town the spot where the King saw fourteen-fifteenths
of his fine troops for the last time.* Here, in the most beautiful
part of our fatherland, we all had a last taste of the good life of
peace. After fifteen days of almost constant parades and inspec-
tions the army corps, under the command of the Crown Prince,†
moved off in four columns, the 'Duke Louis' Chasseurs forming
part of the last. Through Heilbronn, Neustadt, Öhringen and
Künzelsau we marched to Weikersheim. All the time that we
marched through Württemberg we remained uneasily in doubt
as to our destination, fearing that it might yet prove to be a false
alarm. For neither the commanding general nor his deputy,

* The Württemberg contingent numbered about 15,000.
† William, who succeeded his father in 1816 and reigned until 1864.

General von Scheler, had stated categorically that war was inevitable, nor did the newspapers contain any reference to its imminence.

Even at the time of the first order recalling the troops from leave we had anticipated that it was Russia we would be fighting, and the direction of our march confirmed this view. What was still uncertain, however, was whether there would be a war at all. But once we had crossed the borders of our native land we were, at last, convinced. All fears of a return to barracks vanished, our hearts grew lighter, and the troops began to sing on the march.

'Comrades, we're off to Russia!' they sang. Our hopes were high, and though we did not expect to find pots of gold in Russia, we did hope for the best and fastest horses—a cavalryman's fondest dream—and for food and supplies in abundance. No one gave a thought to the Russian winter; no one had any conception of it. A few reflective spirits, it is true, said 'wait and see', but they preached to deaf ears. Yet what purpose would have been served by robbing us of our rosy expectations? Is it not better for a soldier to go into battle gaily rather than to follow his calling in fear and terror of the direst suffering and privations?

So we marched along merrily and were quite content with no more than one day's rest in six. In the archbishopric of Würzburg we found our quarters inferior to those in Württemberg, though the country is richer and more fertile. We missed the most beautiful stretch of the valley of the Main, for, as is customary when great armies are on the march, the more mobile troops kept clear of the main roads. In Würzburg territory this posed no problem, but in the Duchies of Saxony there were not many surfaced roads to choose from. In Hildburghausen I had the honour of reporting our regiment's passage to the reigning Duke. There and in Schleusingen we had our first chance of putting to the test the proverb that Saxon girls are as easy-going as they are pretty, and found it quite apt.

On 23rd March our column passed through the Thuringian mountains. I had been looking forward to seeing these mountain forests and found my highest expectations fulfilled. Not far from Frauenwalde, the loftiest point on the road we travelled, there is a spot from which one of the most beautiful parts of this splendid mountain range with its lofty, thickly-wooded peaks and deep, pleasant valleys is spread before the traveller's eye in infinite variety. The imposing ruins of famous castles such as Gleichenburg and Ilmenburg recall echoes of Germany's past glory. Beyond, at the foot of the range, nestles the pretty little town of Ilmenau. The countryside continues hilly as far as Rudolstadt. As good luck would have it, we rode there along an extravagantly romantic valley through which the river Schwarzach runs, and sometimes rages, past the venerable castle of Schwarzburg before reaching the kingdom of Saxony. Skirting the lovely valley of the Saale we passed through several smaller Saxon towns including Boda, Eisenberg and Krossen and the rather larger Zeitz, reaching the outskirts of Leipzig in the last days of March. There we were allowed a few days of rest and relaxation. There, also, we had our first encounters with the French. We had been warned repeatedly to avoid quarrels with them, but on the very first day some twenty French conscripts out, apparently, to try the Germans' patience, might have provoked a serious incident but for the firmness with which our admirable sergeant-major Beck handled the situation.

Up to this point our expectations, far from being disappointed, had been exceeded. In our native country we had enjoyed good quarters, excellent food and delicious hock to drink. On the march through Würzburg the fare had not been as good, but the famous wine of the Main valley had made up for it. In Thuringia we began to savour Saxon hospitality, and the closer we approached Leipzig the more comfortable did we find our billets. The beautiful Saxon countryside had largely recovered from the ravages of the 1806 war* and good harvests had restored the peasants' prosperity. In the towns we were astonished at the goodwill and warmth we encountered, and the readiness with which we were offered the best that kitchens and cellars could provide. Only the Saxon nobility failed, at times, to live up to this high standard of hospitality. Partly, no doubt, this could be explained by the deep scars the war had left, but I got the impression that some of the titled families I met were being beggared by the prevailing and ever-increasing luxury with which they felt themselves obliged to keep pace. This, and the sharp contrast between some of their villages and those owned by the Crown, left me with a somewhat unfavourable impression of the Saxon gentry. In this respect, at least, they were plainly no better than their brethren elsewhere. There were exceptions, of course, as for instance at Knauthayn, the mansion of Count von Hohenthal near Leipzig where I spent a few days, and in the houses of some others of the highest rank. Complaints of neglect and bad management seemed directed mainly at the lesser nobility.

Our life on the march had been one of harmonious good fellowship. Many amusing anecdotes from the previous night's billets made the rounds of the officers' mess at wayside halts over a good breakfast or luncheon. Not a day passed without

---

* Napoleon's campaign against Prussia and Saxony, culminating in the victory of Jena.

some incident of this kind, and though not all the tales may have been gospel truth they did at least provide entertainment. Our particular favourite was decent, good-natured H*st*n, with his daily amorous adventures and his naïve way of telling them. It was our usual practice to have half the squadron billeted in one village, and on these occasions I shared quarters with Lieutenant K., a most agreeable companion. He was extremely well read and also had a fine singing voice which gave me much pleasure.

So, on our way from Heilbronn to the outskirts of Leipzig, we had passed through much beautiful country, had seen many pretty towns and villages, and had been entertained by a great variety of hosts. One of my pleasantest billets had been with District Commissioner Geisse at Marienhausen, near Hassfurth. My host's friendliness and his wife's motherly care attached me greatly to his family. Others, too—notably at Fröhstockheim in Würzburg country, at Martinwerd near Ilmenau, at Launbach near Rudolstadt and at Unterschweinitz near Zeitz—put me in their debt by the care and attention which they devoted to the well-being of a fellow German. In Count Hohenthal's mansion at Knauthayn I was accorded outstanding hospitality as well as absorbing entertainment from his well-stocked library.

On the occasion of a review by our commander, the Crown Prince, I saw something of the city of Leipzig, Pleissen castle and the handsome collection of Meissen porcelain. Lack of time prevented me from seeing more. Moreover, I felt so much at my ease at Knauthayn that I grudged every moment away from the place. But this state of ease lasted only from 1st to 6th April. An order from the French Emperor summoned us from the delights of Leipzig to Frankfurt-on-the-Oder. We guessed that it would be a long time before we spent so pleasant a week again, for the Saxon countryside beyond Leipzig promised no similar amenities, and even less was to be expected of the March of Brandenburg where, after the events of 1806 and 1807, Württemberg soldiers could hardly expect a very warm welcome.*

* Württemberg joined Napoleon's German allies, the Confederation of the Rhine, in 1806, and a Württemberg contingent took part in the war against Prussia that year. The Württembergers had a reputation for toughness and ruthlessness towards the civilian population of countries through which they passed.

II

O N 7th April we left our quarters, paraded through Leipzig, skirted, on the 9th, the battlefield of Torgau* without, unfortunately, being able to take a closer look at it, saw the fortress, still under construction, and the same day crossed the Elbe. In Torgau those who understood something of such matters admired the bearing and appearance of our regiment.

On the 10th we passed through the pleasant little town of Herzberg and on to Frankenhayn, where the parson entertained us most agreeably with a wealth of anecdotes.

The following day, in billets at Beesdau, the 'Duke Louis' Chasseurs received special and particular orders from the Emperor Napoleon to detach itself from the Württemberg army corps and join the Silesian Lancers and 6th Polish Hussars under the command of Brigadier General Ornano and Major General Watier de St Alphonse. † We were, accordingly, to proceed with all possible speed to Frankfurt to link up with the forces of these two officers. After several hours' march through Lusatia, where the Wendish language which the peasants spoke led to a number of misunderstandings, we entered the March of Brandenburg at Kossenblatt, were inspected for the last time by the Crown Prince at Müllrose and reached Frankfurt-on-the-Oder the same day. Henceforth we had no further contact with the Württemberg corps.

It was, of course, a signal honour for our regiment to be selected by the Emperor for attachment to General Watier's division, which was to form the vanguard of the Grand Army.

* Where Frederick the Great of Prussia defeated the Austrians in 1760. The fortress was begun by Napoleon.

† The division formed part of General Montbrun's Second Corps of the Grand Army's Cavalry reserve, under the overall command of Marshal Murat, King of Naples.

We were very conscious of this distinction and well aware that it would afford us ample opportunity of winning glory and honour on the field of battle. To this extent we had every reason to be satisfied with the French Emperor's dispositions. But on the other hand there was a good deal to be said against joining a French division. French troops, in those days, were apt to regard their comrades of the Rhenish Federation with a good deal of condescension* and even to abuse them at the slightest provocation. This exposed us to the risk of unfortunate incidents from which even the most self-assured of colonels might not always be able to protect his regiment. But first and foremost: however good our relations with the French turned out to be, we would never be able to count on them for the degree of support which we would have expected—and received, time and conditions permitting—from our own army corps. Our severance from our compatriots also gave rise to justified anxiety about the care of our sick and wounded, for we knew a good deal about the negligence, and sometimes downright brutality, with which French doctors were in the habit of treating their patients.† Nor was it

* The French certainly had their doubts about the competence of their Allies. According to one of their cavalry commanders, Colonel Marbot, 'The foreigners' (who made up more than half of the King of Naples' force) 'all served very badly and often paralysed the efforts of the French troops.'

† This looks like a piece of nationalistic prejudice. There is no evidence that French surgeons were either more negligent or more brutal than those of any other European nation. On the other hand those closest to Napoleon testified to his special concern for the wounded. His ordnance officer during the Russian campaign, Baron Gaspar Gourgaud described him as 'of all generals, whether ancient or modern, the one who has paid the greatest attention to the wounded. . . . His first thought after every battle was of them.' And Count Philippe-Paul de Ségur, the Emperor's aide-de-camp during the campaign, movingly describes his distress at the sight of wounded after the battle of Borodino. When a member of his retinue pointed out that

certain, either, how we would get on with the Silesian Lancers, a fact that might have the most serious bearing on our fortunes. The thought of all these problems enabled us to keep our delight at the honour done us within bounds. Had it been for us to choose we would have stayed with our fellow countrymen to share their joys and sorrows.

From Leipzig to Frankfurt our march led us through less prosperous regions. The villages and dwellings of the Lusatians convey no very favourable impression of their affluence, and the interiors of their houses indicate poverty and lack of cleanliness. In the March of Brandenburg we were thoroughly unwelcome guests and there were many complaints about inadequate billets, though often due less to lack of good-will on the part of the inhabitants than to Mother Nature which has treated the region around Frankfurt in the most stepmotherly fashion, endowing it only with vast expanses of barren sand. But the dislike the Frankfurters felt for us also led to several unpleasant incidents.

One of the prettier small towns between Leipzig and Frankfurt is Lübben, with about 6,000 inhabitants. Frankfort itself can be classed as a large town, at any rate to judge by its atmosphere. It lies on the banks of the Oder and is excellently placed for trade and shipping, for the river here is already quite broad and deep. In peacetime it must be the centre of quite a considerable traffic. I had more leisure here than in Leipzig to look about me, and made good use of it. I found little of architectural or cultural interest, nor did I look for much, but concentrated my attention on the lives and habits of the people. Just

---

an injured soldier for whom he was showing solicitude was 'only a Russian' Napoleon replied: 'There are no enemies after a victory, but only men.' Then—Ségur says—'he scattered the officers who were following him over the battlefield to help the wounded whose cries could be heard everywhere.'

as the climate of the March of Brandenburg differs a good deal from that of Southern Germany, so the manners and way of life of its inhabitants show marked contrasts.

The North German is distinguished from the South German by greater polish and address in his manners, but the South German is more open, sincere and honest. Kindliness and good nature are among the foremost traits of the South German character, whereas the North German tends to put his own interest above all else. We are told, to be sure, that our moral standards are constantly declining, but they will have to sink a good deal lower yet before they reach the North German level, at any rate in the towns and cities. It is deeply shocking to be constantly pestered by six- or eight-year-old urchins with offers of introductions to ladies of easy virtue. I suspect that where the rabble is so utterly depraved the middle classes are not likely to be much better and I did in fact, see well-dressed citizens in no way identifiable as foreigners similarly accosted. Nor does this apply to Frankfurt alone, but more or less to all the larger North German towns, and in particular to those where foreign troops —especially French troops—have long been stationed.

The people of Frankfurt were not slow to harrow us with the most dismal stories about Poland, through part of which we were about to pass, but we paid little attention to them, being quite certain in our own minds that we would find ourselves far better provided there than in Brandenburg. We were soon to discover how right the Prussians were, and that their tales of woe were by no means prompted solely by the malice they bore us.

Binninger lith.

III

O N 16th April our new Brigadier General, Ornano, inspected us, expressed himself well satisfied with our bearing and wished us a pleasant journey to Poland. After crossing the Oder we took the Poznan road. That day we passed the battlefield of Kunersdorf* but had no opportunity of inspecting it more closely. From Frankfurt onward the countryside takes on an increasingly bleak and arid appearance, with even sandier soil. It was another two and a half days before we finally bade farewell to Germany, entering the Grand Duchy of Warsaw on 18th April. The first Polish place we came to, the little town of Tzermeissel, we felt must be the most wretched in Poland, but the next was more wretched still, the third yet more desolate, and so on. That night, however, I still had the good fortune to find lodgings in a Benedictine monastery, whose interior did not belie the impression of solid wealth indicated by its handsome façade. The village belonging to it, however, and its inhabitants, seemed miserable in the extreme.

At this place a small stream forms the frontier between Poland and Silesia and on the Silesian side, too, there stands a village which, though nothing to write home about by our standards, nevertheless presented a very marked contrast indeed to that on the Polish side—quite possibly because it was less priest-ridden. 'Wherever you go, it's the same thing with the clergy,' I told myself, but all the same it annoyed me.† I personally was in no position to complain. I was well looked after and given

* At Kunersdorf Frederick the Great of Prussia suffered his most serious defeat of the Seven Years' War at the hands of the Russians and Austrians.

† On this subject, at any rate, Vossler found himself in agreement with Napoleon who, according to the French historian Thiers, described the large number of monasteries in Poland and Russia as 'melancholy symptoms of a low state of civilization'. Unlike Napoleon, Vossler was a Lutheran.

Polish wine which, considering its provenance, was quite passable. My men, on the other hand, ate pickled cabbage and potatoes with the farm hands and drank raw spirits. Even this fare was rather inferior to what we encountered in other Polish villages not blessed with a monastery. Most of the people hereabouts, by the way, still speak German.

Next day we began to move across the vast plain, disfigured here and there by villages whose houses resembled our pig-sties back at home. After eight hours on the march I was detailed to take two squadrons to the village of Löwin for their billets. I asked our guide how far it was, but he was a Pole born and bred and understood me no better than I him. When, after a depressing journey, we finally reached the place there was not a soul who spoke German. Never before had I felt so ill at ease as among these people with whom I could not exchange so much as a word and whose unkempt appearance disgusted me as much as their filthy houses. The foul weather, moreover, compelled me to spend all my time in the sty which they graced with the name of living room. When I remembered my lodgings at Knauthayn I could have wept, but I consoled myself with the thought that I was not alone in my plight and that the whole regiment was in much the same deplorable situation and plagued by the same dirt. It is remarkable how suffering is alleviated by the knowledge that it is shared by others. This day and the next two, on which I experienced similar discomforts, depressed me very much. I was convinced that our condition had reached rock-bottom. Had I but known what was in store for us I would have counted my blessings. The monotony of our march during subsequent days did nothing to raise my spirits, but gradually I became resigned to our new situation and so found it more bearable. I had also, by now, acquired a smattering of Polish which enabled me to conduct the necessary exchanges with my hosts.

In the afternoon of 22nd April we reached the vicinity of Poznan and, to my inexpressible relief, were billeted for a day of rest in villages inhabited by German colonists. The houses in these villages were much better built and the people clean and tidy. I felt almost as if I were back in Germany. The first question I asked my new hosts was how long they had been living here and how they liked it. I was much impressed by their attachment to the land of their fathers which most of them had never seen, though they spoke of it with such fervour and in such detail as if they had spent half their lives there. But I was saddened by their account of their present condition: how bitterly they were hated and sometimes physically ill-treated by the native population and how much they regretted their parents' decision to settle here. Few even among those that were born here spoke the local language, and this may well be one of the reasons why the Poles disliked them and tried to make their lives miserable.

On our day of rest I had time to bring my diary up to date and to reflect once more upon our march through Poland. The assurance of educated Poles I had met that the countryside beyond Poznan was even more wretched did nothing to raise my spirits. So far, to tell the truth, I had had no more than three really bad billets, where I had to share my night's quarters with my hosts and all their familiars, such as pigs, goats, calves, geese, ducks and chickens. In Chelmo, near Pinne, I had lodged at the manor of Count Stanicki, who was not present in person, but whose young sons, accomplished and widely read, gave a favourable impression of their father's cultural standards. As for his moral standards I am not qualified to judge, but his village and his peasants were sadly impoverished. The following day, at the suggestion of my squadron commander, I had been invited for the evening to the home of Count Prujimski. The Count seemed ignorant, silly and exceedingly arrogant. The Countess was a stiff matron, if possible even more snobbish than her husband. The daughter beautiful, with a good figure and quite talented, but excessively vain. There was also a niece, quite passable in appearance, a young widow whose weeds seemed to irk her and who basked in the attentions which a vigorous young lieutenant, also billeted on the Count, lavished upon her.

The old Count's hospitality was genteel but frugal: rare dishes but not half enough to go round, drink that resembled vinegar more than beer served from sparkling goblets and, with the dessert, a thimbleful of Hungarian wine. Before supper the young Countess displayed her considerable musical talents which were much appreciated. But what really delighted her audience was a Cossack dance she performed with her younger sister. We were entranced, and most reluctant to follow the call to supper. Despite the scanty meal I was in excellent spirits which vanished only when, returning to my billet, I passed the miserable hovels which served to house the peasants.

On 24th April I bade a sad farewell to my good German hosts and wished them luck, though I doubt whether they will ever encounter much of it. The regiment assembled at Demsen, another German colonists' village, and paraded through Poznan. The vast number of clattering windmills that surround the town, especially at its western outskirts, amazed us as much as it frightened our horses. The town itself has several handsome streets, built during the German occupation, and in general presents a more attractive appearance than most of its Polish rivals.

Beyond the town we crossed the river Wartha and continued our march towards Gnesen. My squadron commander was billeted that night with the local squire in a village that boasts the unlikely name (I hope I have it right) of Koszalkowikorski. The squire's daughters, so the story went, were engaged to officers of the Polish lancers and had promised their fiancés, when they went to war, that they would not exchange so much as a single word with a strange man. How long they kept their promise I do not know, but can vouch that at least during the Württembergers' stay they did so to the letter, though the squire's bailiff assured us it was a full fortnight since they had made it. We took the ladies for dumb, and even the bailiff's repeated assurances could scarcely persuade us of the contrary.

The following day we reached Gnesen, a sizeable though poorly built town, seat of an archbishop and famous for its horse market. At my billet in Czecznigrolevski I had a very inquisitive landlord who happened to be entertaining an even more prying parson. Both plied me with questions about all the countries through which we had passed, and especially about our own country, its climate, culture and constitution. Neither of the two gentlemen had ever set foot outside the Polish borders or knew much more about his own homeland than that their village was situated in its better part, and that to the south there existed countries which, they suspected, might excel Poland somewhat both as to climate and perhaps even culture. My descriptions were therefore bound to arouse great amazement, and by the time I had spent several hours telling them of the mild climate of Württemberg, its culture, its inhabitants and their way of life, they regarded Southern Germany as a veritable paradise, and me almost with envy. My host was so delighted with my account that he spared neither trouble nor expense to show me how welcome a guest I was. As for me, I had spent a pleasant evening losing myself in happy memories. It was one of the most agreeable days I spent in Poland.

Next day our march took us through several squalid little towns. In one of them (Radezejew) many Württembergers are settled who were overjoyed at the sight of their compatriots, questioning us keenly about their home towns and relatives and giving heart-rending accounts of their deplorable condition in Poland. On 30th April we crossed the Vistula in great barges, left the Grand Duchy of Warsaw on 3rd May and set foot, near Ilienburg (or Illow), on East Prussian soil. On the 6th we moved into temporary quarters at Neidenburg.

Our relief at reaching East Prussia and shaking the dust of Poland from our feet was as unanimous as it was heart-felt. Where formerly we had execrated all Prussia for the boorishness of the Brandenburgers and the inadequacy of their billets, we now thanked God that we were among human beings once more. But I do not want to appear unjust to the Poles, and so I had better insert at this point some observations which are bound to strike any traveller entering Poland and tell a few anecdotes by way of illustration. Perhaps I should preface my remarks by recalling the comfort and thrift to which I had been brought up, and the sense of justice and probity which my good parents had instilled in me. This background probably made me more sensitive about Polish shortcomings than others might have been in my place.

In Poland the nobility is the only part of the nation that counts, and the dominant trait in a Polish nobleman's character is pride. It is a relic of the country's former constitution, under which every nobleman not only had a voice in the election of the King but was himself eligible. In general, the Polish nobleman bullies his servants and cringes before his masters. He is suspicious, malicious and treacherous towards his fellow countrymen and even a common cause will not always ensure his loyalty. He puts his own interests before those of the State, or makes the latter coincide with the former. Poland has always been split into factions, and strong men have been in the habit of supporting one side or the other passionately without ever vouchsafing their country that tranquillity which is so difficult to maintain under an elective monarchy. High living and love of pomp have beggared some families, tempted others into treason, and finally ruined the country. Kosciuszko* and other good men vainly tried to save their country but could not prevent its decay. Poland was dismembered, but the manner in which it was done was hardly calculated to inspire the nation, or rather the nobility, with love for its new status. Though Prussia did her best to put her part of the country on its feet—and traces of these efforts are still agreeably evident—the nobility saw the Prussians only as oppressors and spurned their good intentions They saw their fortunes restored, but as they had no wish to be beholden to their enemies derived no pleasure from the fact. Eagerly they took up arms when Napoleon promised to re-establish the Polish State, recklessly they dissipated their treasure and their blood and hailed the French Emperor as their deliverer. But he, far from keeping his promise, created the Grand Duchy of Warsaw, which he bled white with levies of men and money. But the Poles saw this only as a passing phase and bore

* Polish patriot and statesman who led the Polish rebellion against Russia in 1794 but was defeated as much by disunity within his own ranks as by the combined efforts of Russia, Austria and Prussia. Earlier he had distinguished himself in the American war of independence, being granted the rank of colonel in the revolutionary army.

their burdens patiently. Another war with Russia, they felt certain, would restore Poland to its former glory. On this all their hopes were focussed, and it explained their absolute devotion to Napoleon.*

In the Grand Duchy of Warsaw, ruled by Saxony, the Polish nobility counted for little. A restoration of the kingdom of Poland, they trusted, would also restore to them their lost privileges, their vanished fortunes and their battered prestige. It was the loss of their privileges which they resented most keenly and whose restoration they expected most confidently from that of the kingdom. In Prussian Poland the nobles had regained their prosperity. In the Duchy of Warsaw they stayed poor, though memories of past riches lingered. Whether from a natural bent towards extravagance fostered by education abroad, or because they had never suffered real want, the habit of prudent thrift was alien to their nature. Run-down estates and a constant shortage of cash were the inevitable consequences. Let me cite a few examples: In Cornowa, two days' march beyond Gnesen, I met a squire whose windows were papered over for want of glass, who could not afford enough wood to warm the family parlour, whose face was haggard with hunger but whose daughters

---

* Various reasons have been suggested for Napoleon's failure to keep his promise, among them his fear of offending his ally Austria which occupied a large slice of Polish territory, and his disillusionment with what he saw of the Polish aristocracy during the campaign of 1809. It may be doubted whether his decision in any way affected the outcome of the campaign of 1812. The Polish nobility were deeply committed to his cause in any case, and the common people showed no particular enthusiasm for the French even when the promise still stood. Writing of the 1809 campaign, Captain J.-R. Coignet notes in his recollections: 'We had little to thank the Poles for; they had all run away. All their villages were deserted. They would have allowed a soldier to die at their doors without giving him any help.'

nevertheless dressed in silk and were served by a lady's maid clad in muslin. Another officer of my regiment had a similar experience but even more striking: the greatest imaginable luxury in public combined with such a lack of the most elementary amenities at home that the entire family of nobles drank out of a single glass and used a single fork at a table devoid of linen. For want of bedding and habitable rooms the officers billeted on this gentleman were compelled to sleep on straw, cheek by jowl with his daughters.

There is no middle class in Poland. As for the peasants, they are the slaves of their noble masters and are reared like cattle. They receive no schooling whatever and are trained only in the use of a few simple farm tools. They own no property; they and their land belong to the squire who uses them to work his estates and allows them for their own use a patch barely big enough to support themselves and their families in squalor. They do not benefit from bountiful harvests and depend on his bounty for support when the crops fail. Born and bred a slave, the peasant's wants and aspirations are on the level of the beasts he tends. He submits patiently to his master's most barbarous whims and reverently kisses the boot that kicks him. The inhuman treatment that is commonly his lot leaves him dull and brutish. He hardly dares to breathe in his master's presence. If the latter's generosity has left him with a few coppers to spare he spends them on raw spirits and turns himself from something barely human into a beast. The habit of thieving which is so deeply ingrained in most common Poles (and of which every traveller would do well to beware) is motivated not so much by greed as by the irresistible craving for liquor. Another consequence of this state of slavery is the all-pervading filth encrusting practically every peasant dwelling, spreading like a blight over every aspect of domestic life. Imagine a room consisting of crudely hewn logs laid higgledy-piggledy on top of each other, the cracks stuffed with moss, the warped door secured with a wooden latch, three windows twelve inches high by eighteen wide, one of which is glazed and the other two fitted with wooden shutters, the floor of dried mud, along two of the walls narrow benches flanking a small, splintery wooden table, a circular baking oven with a wooden chimney in a corner, two bunks —one on top of the other—for the humans to sleep in and the rest of the room teeming with half a dozen geese, ducks, chickens, piglets, a goat (a billy-goat if you are unlucky), a calf and a cow. There you have the picture of a Polish farm labourer's cottage and of our troops' billets in Poland.

IV

WE stayed at Neidenburg only three days and were then pushed a further day's march on by the Bavarians following in our rear. Our new encampment was situated between Passenheim and Wartenburg. My lucky star guided me to the house of Squire Freytag in Pattaunen, where I spent twelve very pleasant days. My undemanding tastes and regular habits endeared me greatly to the Freytag family and we parted with mutual regrets. But our days of rest had come to an end, and on 23rd May we moved off, accompanied by the good wishes of these kind people, to yet another encampment, this time near Rössel. Here, with a detachment of twelve men, I was detailed to establish an advanced picket at Goldap. We arrived there on the 26th, passing on our way a beautiful monastery called 'The Holy Linden Tree', the towns of Rastenburg and Angersburg, and several fine state farms, among them Popiollen and Sperling. In Goldap I relieved Lieutenant von Teschen of the Prussian Lancers and found myself manning a headquarters and two outposts. For eight days I stayed with Alderman Reutter von Waldaukadel, a splendid individual who was mayor and chief magistrate of the town and of whom I grew so fond that I found our parting quite a wrench. I had met among the East Prussians with more goodwill, sincerity and true friendliness than among the Brandenburgers. That part of East Prussia which I had seen so far is generally very fertile, and the people, both in the towns and on the land, lead comfortable if not affluent lives and are of a carefree disposition. The towns are solidly built and some of the houses might even be described as elegant. What especially took my fancy were the large market squares, which they call circuses, and by which the inhabitants set great store. The villages make a somewhat threadbare impression, without being in any way really poor, and are generally clean.

V

S O far, with the exception of our march through Poland, things had gone well with me. In the whole of my previous existence I had experienced only a few days of suffering and none of real anguish. But from now on I was to witness and, indeed, experience scenes of every imaginable distress, wretchedness and misery. No thought of this, however, yet entered my mind. Our golden dreams of Russia, to be sure, had been tarnished by the tales of Poles and Prussians, and had given way to soberer reflections, but neither I nor my comrades had even the faintest idea of the horrors in store for us.

Yet it was with a somewhat heavier heart that I set out for Olesko on 4th June. I rejoined my regiment a few days later and on the 14th crossed the frontier into the Duchy of Warsaw for the second time. We were granted a few more days of rest in Wärbellen, which we employed in foraging for supplies in the neighbourhood. By order of the Emperor each regiment was to provide itself with twenty-three days' rations. Heavily armed detachments combed the whole of this part of the Duchy, ransacking houses, taking whatever food they could find and leaving the inhabitants with no more than eight days' supplies. I, too, found myself in charge of one of these abominable patrols and to this day shudder at the memory of it. Eight days later, at the crossing of the Niemen, the greater part of this plunder was abandoned, whether in compliance with orders from on high or at the behest of the French commissariat I do not know. One thing, however, is certain: these vast supplies were later sold for a great deal of money.*

* This sacking of the Polish and Lithuanian countryside caused great indignation. Though Napoleon had issued orders for wholesale requisitioning, the way in which it was carried out shocked him and he reprimanded the commanders of some of the Allied contingents sharply for their lack of dis-

On 18th June the Grand Army began to concentrate and vast masses of troops moved ponderously towards the Niemen. A small diversion was provided by a parade of more than 10,000 cavalry before Major-General Montbrun near Marienthal, but that very same day we thought the campaign had begun with us in the lead when we were made to advance at the trot for two solid hours. On 22nd and 23rd June a veritable torrent of troops at last rolled forward across the immense plain to the very banks of the river, which formed the frontier with Russia, and there awaited the order to cross.* For days past the French army had left a swath of pillage and destruction in its wake as it moved through friendly territory. Heaven only knew what it would do on enemy soil!

On the evening of the 23rd two pontoon bridges were thrown across the river, without much interference from the enemy, an

---

* The Grand Army consisted of more than 600,000 men of whom about 325,000 crossed the Niemen into Russia at this point. Six months later, 1,000 armed troops and some 20,000 stragglers re-crossed the river into Poland. Of the 1,250 guns with which they had set out they brought back 9.

---

cipline. Ségur, while admitting that the French had taught their Allies to live off the countryside, complained somewhat naïvely that 'the coarse and clumsy manner in which they did it shocked us all'. As a result of much confusion at the crossing of the Niemen, and of the subsequent rapid advance of the Army, practically all these vast supplies were dissipated, though a good part of them was dragged a considerable distance into Russia. Vossler's comment that they were later sold for a great deal of money sounds like hearsay, but his criticism of the rapacious French commissariat was echoed by other Württembergers who took part in the campaign. Most of them, however, emphasize that Napoleon himself knew nothing of this and would have disapproved if he had.

hour's march upstream from Kowno, and several cavalry regiments crossed over to the other side.

At dawn on the 24th the main body of the Grand Army began to cross the fatal river. It was a glorious morning, but by afternoon a violent thunderstorm began to gather and soon the rain came pelting down in buckets.* In two days and nights, during which each regiment and corps seemed to be treading on the heels of the other, the passage of the river was completed.

General Watier de St Alphonse's division formed the vanguard and in two and a half days marched through three villages as far as Zobiliski, half-way to Troki. A few enemy patrols we encountered on our way made off speedily without risking an engagement. On the evening of the 26th there were many more of them but they, too, melted away when we prepared to attack them. On the 27th the whole army regrouped for a battle with the Russian main force at Vilna, but the Russians merely set fire to the city's warehouses, destroyed the bridge across the Vilna river and allowed the Grand Army to enter the place practically unopposed on the 29th. The Grand Army now pressed on with all possible speed along two roads to catch up with the elusive Russians, who were retiring towards Dünaburg. Our division used a minor road which led through Vidzy and Braslaw. Every day the enemy's light horse seemed on the point of making a stand and did, in fact, engage us in occasional skirmishes. Losses on both sides were negligible, but the Russians achieved their aim of slowing our advance. On 4th July we were to have had a day of rest near Swinsiany; and on

* This sudden break in the weather caused heavy losses in horses and other livestock and brought on widespread sickness among the troops.

this day the Russians launched a more concerted attack with the result that we lost at least half of our rest day.*

Very early on 5th July our corps resumed its march and half an hour later made contact once again with the enemy who was adjusting the speed of his retreat to our pace. We rushed at them but the enemy rearguard were just as quick to vanish, leaving a few patrols on either side of the road to harry us. After five hours of constant skirmishes and teasing by the Russians we arrived very tired at the top of a slope where General Wittgenstein and Duke Alexander of Württemberg † had taken up positions near the village of Daugelisky, where a marshy stream and an expanse of swamp and scrub made the mounting of an attack particularly hazardous. The King of Naples, who had assumed command of the entire corps of cavalry two days previously, moved our brigade forward to spearhead the attack, siting it for the time being in the line of some well-aimed Russian gunfire.‡ However, when he became aware of the difficulties of the terrain he gave the order to retreat so as to give men and horses a chance to gather their strength and in order to reconnoitre the enemy positions. A party of skirmishers meanwhile kept the Russians occupied. The attack was to begin at four o'clock in the afternoon. Colonel von Waldburg addressed his

---

* The Russian tactics of wearing out the Grand Army's vanguard by constant skirmishing without ever risking a major engagement were highly successful. Between the Niemen and the Dvina the Army lost, from exhaustion and disease, nearly a quarter of its effective strength without having fought a single battle.

† One of the King of Württemberg's brothers who commanded a Russian division.

‡ Marshal Murat was a dashing and surpassingly brave cavalry officer but no general.

regiment with a few firm, well-chosen words, reminding it of its past record and urging it to show its mettle. None of us doubted for one moment that we would capture the enemy battery which was our objective.

At the head of the brigade the 'Duke Louis' Chasseurs skirted the swamps by way of some thick scrub, regained the road, galloped full tilt through heavy Russian cannon fire across the bridge spanning a stream at the foot of the enemy redoubt and formed up on the other side for the assault. Quickly the Russian artillery retreated behind a regiment of dragoons who awaited our charge. But when it came they broke almost immediately, as did the second regiment behind them. A third one, however, stood its ground and finally forced our cavalry, which looked back anxiously and vainly for support, to retreat. This compelled our regiment's fourth squadron—my squadron—which, covering the right wing, had beaten back several squadrons of Cossacks, to withdraw also. Now, at long last, the two remaining regiments of the brigade arrived, but it was too late, and all we gained from this gallant charge were a few enemy prisoners and captured horses while on our side Lieutenant Colonel Prince Hohenlohe fell into enemy hands. The Russians, however, decided not to await a second attack and quickly withdrew. Half an hour later the King of Naples inspected the regiment, honoured it, as he rode along the lines, with the exclamation: 'Foundre, vous avez bien chargé!' and promised glittering rewards which, however, never materialized. On this day and the next we welcomed many deserters to our lines, mostly from Russian Poland.

Our losses that day were insignificant, and those of the Russians, which were very heavy, especially in horses, the more remarkable. On the other hand this engagement reminded us that

Faber du Faur del.

the Russians were quite capable of standing their ground when they were so minded. The necessity to restore several burnt bridges afforded us a day of rest at Daugelisky and another, on the 8th, at Vidzy, with only small detachments of light cavalry on the move reconnoitring the terrain and the enemy positions.

On the 10th we reached Braslaw, about one and a half days' march from Dünaburg. After another day of rest due, presumably, to uncertainty about the enemy's strength, we wheeled right towards Druya and reached the vicinity of this town and of the Dvina river on the evening of the 13th. The following day Druya was abandoned by the Russian cavalry corps which had been moving parallel to our line of march, and since no one knew where it had gone or what its strength was, the division withdrew towards Ikossen, where it was joined by a second division before resuming its advance towards the Dvina the following day. Up to and including the 20th of July these two divisions were engaged in feints and diversions against the Dvina until the Grand Army had concentrated near Dissna. The ultimate aim was to pursue the main body of the enemy who, after abandoning the Dünaburg redoubts, had the choice of withdrawing in the direction of Moscow or of St Petersburg, and to bring him to battle.

On 21st July we rejoined the Grand Army near Dissna and the following day a cavalry corps of some eighteen regiments was ferried across to the right bank of the Dvina.

Thus far the Russian army had withdrawn without accepting a single serious engagement. The rare skirmishes in which it became involved were without any strategic importance. Many of our hot-heads began to fear that peace might be concluded without the Russians even once being brought to battle.

D

The Russian plan of campaign does not seem to have envisaged the defence of their part of Poland, but it certainly included its devastation. Wherever we went we found the houses burnt down and their inhabitants chased into the depths of the forests, leaving nothing behind but smoking ruins. The cattle had either been driven off by the Russians, or removed by the peasants. All stores and provisions for man and beast had been hidden or burnt, and this year's grain harvest, of course, was nowhere near ripe yet for cutting. Only in Vilna had we found any forage, but this was immediately earmarked for the regiments of the Guard, which followed the main army in easy daily stages.*

This devastation obviously raised severe obstacles to the rapid progress of the Grand Army, which were further aggravated by the nature of the country itself. Most of the road from the Niemen to Vilna and some fifteen hours' march beyond is either so sandy or so marshy that even in the most favourable weather conditions it presents great problems to the passage of heavy wagons and equipment. These difficulties are multiplied almost beyond endurance on the short but correspondingly steep slopes of the many ravines which the road crosses at right angles. To cap it all, the weather seemed to be doing its best to contribute to our discomfiture. Before crossing the Niemen we had been thoroughly parched by the persistent oppressive heat. Thereafter we endured three days of continuous and torrential rain followed by alternating periods of unbearable heat and

* Ségur confirms that on one occasion—at Vitebsk—supplies earmarked for other units were diverted to Napoleon's élite force, the Guard, which was kept carefully in reserve throughout the march. This caused discontent in the rest of the Army and may be the occasion to which Vossler refers.

downpours the like of which I had never experienced. To sum
up, our situation was this: we were embarked on a strenuous
campaign entailing frequent forced marches along abominable
roads, either smothered in sand or knee-deep in mud and frequently pitted by precipitous gulleys, under skies alternately un-
bearably hot or pouring forth freezing rain. Our laboriously and
often humiliatingly acquired provisions had become a prey to
the French commissariat at the crossing of the Niemen, many
regiments had no more than three days' supply of rations
which, because of the total devastation of the countryside, could
never be adequately replenished. Four-fifths of the army subsisted on the flesh of exhausted, starving cattle, of which each
regiment dragged at least one herd with it.* Our drink consisted
—not even of inferior spirits or at least wholesome water, but of
a brackish liquid scooped from stinking wells and putrid ponds.
Under these circumstances it was not surprising that within two
or three days of crossing the Niemen the army, and in particular the infantry, was being ravaged by a variety of diseases,
chief among them dysentery, ague and typhus.† To make
matters worse, there was a great shortage of fodder for the

* It has been suggested that Napoleon deferred the opening of the campaign until comparatively late in the season in order to allow for the growth
of grazing for these vast herds of cattle and the draft animals required to
move his artillery and train.

† According to Ségur, the French attributed this devastating outbreak of
dysentery to the troops' habit of cooking their rye flour and eating it as gruel
instead of baking it and eating it as bread. Vossler's suggestion that it was
caused by impure water sounds more likely and is supported by the diaries of
doctors. Ségur also says that the German contingents, 'less alert and less ab-
stemious than the French, and also less involved in a cause that was not
theirs, were the first to succumb' to typhus and dysentery. The Russians
were apparently not seriously affected by the disease.

horses,* which previously had been accustomed to the best. Now they had to make do with green-mown grain and on this diet were required to endure the greatest exertions in all kinds of weather. Even before Vilna hundreds had fallen by the wayside from exhaustion, and by the time the army reached the Dvina it was thousands of horses short. All these circumstances not only weakened the army but led also, of course, to a slackening of discipline which gradually, and in proportion to the exertions demanded of them, resulted in the complete dissolution of entire regiments and divisions. Inexorably the whole vast host seemed to be moving ponderously towards disaster, but everyone clung to the belief that the conquest of one or other of the two capitals, St Petersburg or Moscow, must lead to peace and to the reprieve of what remained of the army.

In this condition, and with these hopes, but with our numbers reduced by nearly one in ten,† the Grand Army massed on 22nd July in the neighbourhood of Dissna and on the shores of the Dvina. I had crossed the Niemen in a state of tense expectation. Now our move into enemy territory proper filled me with nothing but sombre forebodings. But we were an army hundreds of thousands strong, comrades in arms all in the flower of manhood, and many still rejoiced as they crossed the fateful river. On the far bank an ominous silence awaited them. Dense and menacing forests met the eye in every direction. The rare villages were deserted. Not a sign of human life anywhere. The fate of this huge army to which I belonged oppressed me profoundly.

* Though food supplies were on the whole well organized from the Oder as far as the Niemen, fodder, more difficult to transport, was lacking even in the early stages of the campaign. Apart from the draft animals, there were more than 100,000 horses for the cavalry and artillery.

† A considerable under-estimate, according to most other sources.

But to revert for a moment to my own experiences during this stage of the campaign: at the crossing of the Niemen I had the honour of being seconded to General Montbrun's personal service—an honour which, in view of my halting French, I would gladly have forgone. The secondment, however, lasted a mere three days during which I got precious little rest. I spent the days either in the General's retinue or delivering messages and orders, riding myself and my horses to a standstill. The first night found me in pouring rain by a dying camp fire, without food or drink, silently cursing my French comrades who had plenty of both but were in no mood to share it. The second night passed in delivering a message to the King of Naples, at whose headquarters I was at least served with a decent meal.

On the 26th I returned to my regiment, but a mere three days later it was my turn to take charge of the baggage. The corps advanced rapidly. I, with my heavy wagons and worn-out horses, followed more slowly along roads churned up by driving rain. Sometimes horses and wagons got stuck for hours on end in the ravines, blocking the way of those that followed, and during the next four days I never once caught up with my regiment. At last, on the evening of 4th July, after the most prodigious exertions (which my commanding officer seemed barely to appreciate) I regained contact and could consider myself lucky to have lost no more than a third of my stores and equipment for want of horse power. I would have liked to spend some time in Vilna, but with my wagons it was neither expedient nor safe to do so, nor would it have served any practical purpose, for no provisions were to be had from the frightened inhabitants even for good money.

VI

ON 22nd July one cavalry corps, to which my regiment be-longed, crossed the Dvina near Dissna. Several attempts to bridge the river had been frustrated by its swift current and rocky bed. We swam across in columns but lost a fair number of riders and many more horses. We now took the road to Polotsk, which we reached the following day without having encountered any significant enemy resistance. Only on the evening of the 24th, as we approached Vitebsk, did we sight hostile columns which quickly withdrew again. The 25th also provided no more than minor skirmishes, but on the next day the Russians stood their ground and we were able to resume our march towards Vitebsk only after some heavy fighting.

On the far shore of the Dvina the battle of Vitebsk took place on 26th and 27th July, the Russians deploying considerable forces and fighting stubbornly. On the 28th we resumed our march for two hours downstream, swam across the river once more, advanced over the Vitebsk battlefield, swam across the river Ulla and passed through the town of Vitebsk. Without a pause we continued along the narrow road towards Smolensk and reached Liozno on the 29th. A day's rest, and we advanced with the Sebastiani division as far as Rudnya, following up the next day, 1st August, to Inkovo. A reconnaissance undertaken on the 3rd decided the General to remain there until the 6th, when the enemy reappeared and induced the General to re-treat about an hour's march to Lendzi, to take up a more fav-ourable position there. But the next day more Russians were sighted, and on 8th August they fell upon the division, which was seven regiments strong, in greatly superior numbers and forced it to fall back on General Montbrun's corps near Rudnya after a sharp engagement in which our regimental commander, Count von Waldburg, and his adjutant, von Batz, were wounded and taken prisoners.*

There we remained, constantly harrassed but never frontally attacked by the enemy, until 13th August. While we were guarding the army's flank on this side, the remaining corps had gradually gathered in and around Vitebsk. Several days of rest were to freshen the troops to enable them to fall on the enemy with renewed vigour. Though food was scarce, rest and good weather did something to improve their health and spirits.

East of the Dvina the countryside bore a somewhat more friendly aspect: fewer forests and marshes, more cultivated land, better-looking and more numerous villages, more and prettier little towns, and even some bigger ones. Here the retreating Russians had ceased to lay waste the countryside, contenting themselves with destroying all stocks of food and removing most of the inhabitants with their goods and chattels. The weather had become more settled, and with it the roads more passable. As a result, the army lost fewer men and horses than on the march from the Niemen to the Dvina.

From the time we crossed the Dvina until the engagement at Lendzi on 8th August I fared excellently, and could count myself very lucky to have suffered no injury during the hand-to-hand fighting in this battle. A withdrawal such as we carried out on this occasion can almost be regarded as a victory, for despite his immense superiority the enemy did not at any time succeed in breaking our ranks. Even during our retreat through our encampment, where many of the tents were still standing and the guy-ropes constantly tripped us up, our troops never faltered. And in fact nothing short of such steadiness could have

* This was quite a sharp set-back for the French, the Sebastiani division being overwhelmed by 10,000 Russian cavalry.

saved us. As it was, the day's work had cost my regiment its entire stores and rations, and the days of recuperation in the bivouac at Rudnya became days of hunger and privation for us. Whatever vigour and strength men and horses managed to store up were dissipated during this so-called period of rest, for our regiment was quartered on the forward fringe of the Grand Army, had to be ready to move at a moment's notice and to stand by mounted every morning from half-past one until five o'clock to guard against a surprise attack by the enemy.

VII

TOWARDS the middle of August, when it became clear that the Russians were withdrawing towards Moscow, the Grand Army broke camp around Vitebsk, advanced on Smolensk, took the city by storm, fought a bloody battle in the so-called holy valley* and advanced, under constant skirmishing, to the outskirts of Mozhaisk which it reached on 4th September. Here the Russians had taken up prepared positions, which they appeared determined to defend to the last. Here the fate of Moscow was to be decided. On 5th September we succeeded, after great carnage, in taking an enemy redoubt † whose loss gravely imperilled the Russian position. Since the Russian commander could hardly abandon the country's second capital without having fought a decisive battle, he made a tremendous effort to regain the lost redoubt, but in vain. On 6th September both armies rested, while at the same time preparing for the bloody spectacle which the following day was to witness.‡

On 13th August our division broke camp at Rudnya and marched back to Liozno, spending the following week covering the left wing of the Grand Army with marches and countermarches. Nowhere did we encounter any significant bodies of enemy troops. On the 21st we received orders relieving us of this assignment and sending us back, via Inkovo and Lendzi, to Liozno, where we were to deal with partisans harassing the army's

* The battle of Valutina, on 14th August. This was not a happy day for the Württemberg cavalry. Marshal Junot, hard pressed, complained that they were too weakened and spiritless to counter-attack. Vossler's regiment, however, was not involved, as his brief reference to the battle shows. It had, it will be remembered, been detached from the main Württemberg contingent.

† This was the Shevardino Redoubt, intended to be a mere check to the French, but defended by the Russians as if it were Moscow itself.

‡ The battle of Borodino.

rear. Having achieved our objective without much trouble we moved up the line again through Babinowieszi and Usjanikowicz towards Smolensk, but before reaching it wheeled left in the direction of Parezia, and crossed the Dnieper at Dogorobuzh on the main Smolensk–Moscow road. Thence we followed the Grand Army in a series of forced marches through Viazma and Gzhaisk, catching up with it on the eve of the battle of Mozhaisk.

During the whole of this period of rapid movement from 13th August to 6th September we had no encounter of any consequence with the enemy, and only a few forays against our van and rear by skirmishers and irregulars betrayed his presence. Some of the territory we crossed in dealing with the partisans lay off the Grand Army's main line of march and was therefore still partly inhabited. However, the peasants had hidden away most of their belongings and we made no more booty than we needed to supply our small corps with enough rations for a few days. The peasants, for their part, showed a very natural reluctance to have anything to do with us and we established no contact with them whatever. The countryside adjoining the main road, along which our army was advancing, was deserted even before we arrived. Apart from some objects too heavy to carry away, such as great hogsheads of spirits, etc., we found no supplies or provisions of any kind. On our march from Dogorobuzh along the high road to rejoin the main army we found everything devastated. The towns through which we passed had already been taken over by the French administration, which spread itself comfortably over the houses still standing and the many and sometimes very beautiful convents and churches. The weather so far had been good. During August there had been some very hot days, but the nights were already turning cool—

even cold. These sharp changes in temperature were beginning
to affect our health and, to a much greater degree, that of the
army as a whole. From Dogorobuzh onward we met many,
sometimes very many, soldiers who had dropped by the roadside from sheer exhaustion and had died where they lay for lack
of help. In view of our rapid advance by forced marches, and of
the utter devastation once again left behind by the Russians
from Smolensk onward, it would have been impossible, with the
best will and the best organization in the world, to establish
field hospitals for the sick and exhausted. The horses were in no
better shape than the men. Accustomed to good oats, they had
had to make do for weeks past with green rye which had
not made them noticeably leaner but had undermined their
strength. After a hard ride they succumbed in their hundreds.
We found them lying by the roadside in droves and the sight of
them much increased our forebodings about the state of the
Grand Army's cavalry and artillery.

On rejoining the main body of the army on the evening of 6th
September we found it in good and sanguine spirits. The proximity of Moscow, the end to our hardships which everyone expected as a result of its capture, with some no doubt the hope of
plunder and with others the prospect of military distinction
which the next day would provide in plenty, all these thoughts
had helped to stir the emotions, and as we rode into camp we
were congratulated on all sides upon our timely arrival. The
whole army seemed alive with a cheerful bustle, and if one dis-
counted the pale, worn faces of the soldiers he could fancy himself in a camp replete to the point of abundance. Most of the
troops were busily polishing and preparing weapons for the
morrow, and the order reached us to make an early night of it
so as to be ready for the morning's work. Many a soldier stretched

himself out carefree and contented, little thinking that this would be his last night on earth, but one thought was common to us all: things could not go on much longer as they were, the capture of Moscow must bring about an improvement, and if not, then death would be preferable to our present state. Though the numerical strength of the army had shrunk quite alarmingly, the very considerable forces that remained consisted of the strongest and most experienced troops, and the bold and fiery eyes peering from haggard faces promised certain victory.

Returning to my own affairs: nothing of any note had happened to me since 13th August. I shared my regiment's joys and sorrows; at first in want, then in abundance—or what passed as such; that is to say a barely adequate supply of vodka, meat and bread—and finally back again to a lack of even the most elementary necessities of life. I rejoined the Grand Army in good health, but pretty weak and without any provisions. A miserable plateful of bread soup oiled with the stump of a tallow candle was all I had to eat on the eve of the big battle. But in my famished condition even this revolting dish seemed quite appetizing. I ate it gratefully, lay down to rest and slept, like the others, as peacefully as if the coming day was to have resembled its fellows as one egg does another.

At break of day the whole army was astir. Already a few shots could be heard. The regiment mounted and joined the two others of the brigade. A French aide-de-camp appeared bearing a piece of paper inscribed with Napoleon's brief but inspiring proclamation to his army, which the colonel read out to us. The Emperor reminded his troops of their past victories and forecast that victory in the impending battle and the capture of Moscow would put an end to our tribulations. The message was received with universal acclaim.* Presently the boom of cannon could be heard and the battle began. The thunder of artillery came from all sides, at times even drowning the rattle of musketry. We formed up, began our advance, and were greeted initially by no more than a few Russian cannon balls. Ahead of us hand-to-hand fighting had become general and soon we found ourselves subjected to a veritable hail of grapeshot. A regiment of Polish lancers broke under the fire, passing through us before it could be halted. We were on the point of charging, but the enemy recoiled without waiting for the impact, leaving grapeshot from one side and solid cannon balls from the other to tear through our ranks. In front of us a ravine had been taken by our troops. Quickly we followed in their tracks, finding at the bottom some brief shelter from the murderous fire. But when we breasted the far side we were hit at even closer range and with greater intensity. There was nothing for it but to advance as rapidly as we could. Now the enemy cavalry launched a series of attacks, but we stood our ground, while on either side the infantry struggled in fearful carnage. For half an hour we were exposed to this murderous fire before we could attempt to move forward again. But our way was barred by great masses of cavalry against which we would have stood little chance. In the nick of time twenty-four pieces of cannon came to our aid and played their fire on the massed enemy. New regiments came to our support and with their aid we beat back a number of attacks. But

* Napoleon's proclamation read: 'Soldiers, the time for the battle you have so long desired is at hand. Victory now depends on you. It is indispensable for us, it will ensure us all we need, good winter quarters and a speedy return home. Bear yourselves as you did at Austerlitz, Friedland, Vitebsk and Smolensk. Let remotest posterity recall with pride your deeds of valour on this day. Let it be said of each of you: "He was at the great battle under the walls of Moscow".'

still the enemy's artillery was wreaking havoc in our ranks. At last the main Russian positions were taken and the enemy army began to retreat. The cannons and cavalry facing us gradually melted away and the fire of cannon and grapeshot abated. Only one battery of six guns kept up its fire on our flank, and in a copse to our front a detachment of Russian chasseurs held on, seemingly concentrating their fire on the officers. A captain at my side was wounded and at almost the same moment I was hit by a ricochet on the brass band of my helmet and knocked unconscious. However, the battle had been won, and the regiment rode only one more attack after I received my injury.*

The time was half-past five in the afternoon when my wound forced me to leave the field of battle. Four other officers of the regiment had shared my fate that day, and one had been killed. Of the 180 men the regiment had been able to muster that morning half were either dead or wounded. The general commanding the division, General Watier, and the brigadier of our brigade as well as both their seconds-in-command had been wounded, and another senior divisional staff officer killed. The corps commander, General Montbrun, was killed by a howitzer.

The trophies from the battle were meagre. Barely a few hundred prisoners and not a single serviceable cannon fell into our hands. The Russians had fought with great courage and tenacity; many of them were drunk. Eight hundred cannon had been deployed by the two armies to scatter death and destruc-

---

* The Württemberg cavalry distinguished itself in the fighting for the Semyonovskaya Redoubt on the French right, and the regiment under command of General Montbrun's Corps at the Great (Raevski) Redoubt in the centre, which changed hands repeatedly. It was here that Montbrun was killed. The Russian losses in the battle of Borodino were 44,000 men, those of the French not less than 28,000.

tion. Losses in dead and wounded on both sides amounted to more than 40,000 men. The Russians withdrew defeated, but by no means routed.

I was taken to the Württemberg dressing station. On my way I passed the Emperor. He seemed somewhat cold and aloof.* Perhaps he had been looking forward to a more resounding victory. Our regimental surgeon, Doctor Roos,† dressed my wound. I saw many old acquaintances, all more or less seriously wounded, several maimed, some having already drawn their last breath. Supported by a trooper I moved farther to the rear, and was lucky enough to be able to buy a little bread and brandy for the price of two Prussian thalers. With other wounded Württembergers I spent the night in a barn, from where we were taken next morning to the village of Elina, half an hour's ride to the rear of the battlefield. Here the Württemberg wounded were billeted in a number of houses pending their recovery. For the first time in more than two months I had a solid roof over my head again. Since 21st June I had spent my nights either under the open sky or in thatched hovels. Many times I lay on the bare ground while above me the skies opened to release the rain in buckets, often my clothes did not dry on me for days on end. Because of the ubiquitous and inescapable filth I had repeatedly found myself infested with vermin. Since crossing the Niemen I had rarely had enough to eat. There was a shortage of bread

* Nearly all eye-witnesses have commented on Napoleon's lethargic behaviour during the battle of Borodino. He was suffering from a heavy cold and his general state of health was poor.

† Major Heinrich von Roos was senior doctor with Vossler's regiment. His first-aid post at the beginning of the battle was in the ravine in front of the Great Redoubt. He withdrew farther to the rear when it came under fire. Major Roos also kept a diary of his experiences in Russia which was published in 1832.

from the very beginning of the campaign and we subsisted almost entirely on beef and inferior vodka. Occasionally I managed to get hold of some bread, but as a rule it was a concoction of badly-ground flour and great quantities of rye chaff, so that palate and stomach were equally repelled by it and swallowing it presented considerable discomfort and some danger. As a result of this wretched diet and the stale, brackish water scooped from infected wells and pools I succumbed, between Vilna and the Dvina, to repeated bouts of diarrhoea which so sapped my strength that I could hardly mount my horse unaided. After a week or two the diarrhoea abated, but my weakness persisted. My horses had been much exhausted by our many forced marches, and the green-mown rye did not provide them with enough nourishment to restore their energies from day to day. Thus I had lost, long before the battle of Mozhaisk, every one of the horses with which I had crossed the Niemen. A scruffy Cossack pony had become my general purpose mount and my servant's and baggage's transport was reduced to spavined Russian cart horses.

VIII

IN the village of Elina I shared a house with eight other wounded officers. We were bedded on the floor which was covered with some of the thatch pulled out of the roof. Proper food for the sick and wounded was utterly lacking and we subsisted on a weak broth made of stale, lean meat of which a few scraps floated on top, and almost uneatable bread. Medical supplies were practically non-existent. After thirty-six hours my head wound reduced me to a state of stupor in which I remained for a week. My companions in misfortune, all more or less seriously injured, filled the room with their groans and at night deprived me of what little sleep my condition allowed. On the 16th, the hospital was moved back another hour's march from the battlefield, to the manor house of Selsokarazhin. Here there was more room, the sick could be separated from the wounded and the latter quartered in lighter and more cheerful surroundings. I had recovered from my stupor, was classified as lightly wounded and shared with Lieutenant S. a room which would have been quite tolerable but for the many broken window panes. This defect robbed us of our rest from about midnight onward, as we had the greatest difficulty in keeping even bearably warm. We spent our days either sitting in front of the stove and keeping the fire going, or visiting other wounded who were confined to their beds. We spent many cheerful hours with Lieutenant von H., who had lost a foot but none of his gaiety and wit. I whiled away much of the time bringing my diary up to date, though my room-mate's garrulous disposition made this something of an effort. The food, as a rule, was still totally inadequate, though after the capture of Moscow we did, occasionally, get some supplementary rations.

On the 5th we were alarmed by the appearance of a band of

E

so-called peasant Cossacks.* After some initial confusion order was quickly restored and every man armed himself as well as his wounds allowed to ward off the attack. Though this turned out to be a false alarm we thought it advisable to move out of the manor house and back to our former quarters. But there the accommodation was so poor and the danger of the spread of typhoid so serious that it was plain we would have to move out as soon as possible. The hospital commandant, hearing of a well-built village only one and a half hour's ride away on the far side of the battlefield, which had been occupied by our light cavalry but was now abandoned, decided to send out a picket to inspect it. I, as the least seriously wounded, was entrusted with this task.

Early in the morning of the 6th I set out, accompanied by a trooper, and soon reached the battlefield. At first the corpses lay singly, then in heaps. Often my horse could not find a way

* The Cossacks played a vital part in the defeat of the Grand Army. Operating largely independently of the main Russian forces, though in close liaison with them, they constantly harassed the invaders and greatly restricted their scope for manoeuvre. Natives mainly of the Don and Volga they lived in semi-independence, under their own laws and exempt from taxes. They were, however, under an obligation to serve for five years in the Russian army. From early childhood they rode bareback on half-wild horses over the Steppe and were the real guerrilla forces of the Russian campaign. What the Cossacks lacked was a grasp of large-scale organization. The Russian general Count Benckendorff wrote: 'The Cossack is born with that degree of activity, intelligence and enterprise that up to the rank of N.C.O. he is unrivalled; but he degenerates immediately when he is pushed beyond his place into a higher grade.' The 'peasant Cossacks' to whom Vossler refers were probably not genuine Cossacks but bands of partisans recruited from among the peasants in the overrun territories, whose sorties were less organized but for that very reason perhaps even more of a menace to the retreating army.

through them and I had to ride over the bodies. I reached the hill where the redoubt had covered the Russian army's left flank.* Many lives had been lost before its fate had been sealed. Without pausing I continued to thread my way through the corpses, the horror of the scene mounting as I progressed. Soon I reached the redoubt that marked the approximate centre of the battlefield.† Here the corpses lay piled higher and ever higher around a position that had changed hands again and again. The ditches were filled to the brim with bodies. The Württemberg infantry had been in the very thick of this part of the battle and I found bodies in Württemberg uniform by the hundred. The top of these fortifications provided a comprehensive view of almost the entire field of battle. Sword and shot had raged terribly everywhere. Men and horses had been gashed and maimed in every conceivable way, and on the faces of the fallen Frenchmen you could still discern the various emotions in which death had overtaken them: courage, desperation, defiance, cold, unbearable pain; and among the Russians passionate fury, apathy and stupor. The Russian positions had been excellently chosen and only the utmost exertions of the French and their allies had succeeded in driving the enemy from them. The vast mass of corpses bore eloquent testimony to the terrible and solemn drama here enacted and to the awful harvest Death had reaped. For a long time my gaze stayed riveted to the fearful sight which seared my soul so that I shall not forget it until my dying day. At last, with a shudder, I averted my eyes from the scene and perceived, in the very centre of the redoubt, a wooden cross which until then had not caught my eye. I approached and read the following inscription.

* The Semyonovskaya Redoubts.
† The Great Redoubt.

Here lies
GENERAL MONTBRUN
Passer-by of whatever nation,
honour his ashes,
They are the remains of one
of the Bravest of the Brave,
of General Montbrun.
The Duke of Danzig,* Marshal of France,
has erected this modest monument in his honour.
His memory will live for ever in the hearts
of the Great Army.†

So this was where my dear and gracious general had found his last resting place, a man as kind and considerate to his subordinates as he had been brave in war; who had faced death a hundred times and won all his honours and decorations on the field of battle, yet had miraculously escaped injury until the day of his death. A fine and noble person in the flower of his manhood.

I tore myself away, having seen more than enough. Rapidly I crossed the rest of the battlefield and after an hour's hard ride reached the village I was looking for. A few inhabitants had returned and watched me covertly. I had been warned to exercise the greatest caution if I met villagers, for it had become a matter of common knowledge that individual soldiers were often waylaid and murdered by them. Having examined the lay-out of the village and the structure of its houses, and watched the

---

* Marshal Lefebvre, Commander of the Old Guard.

† Çi git / Le Général Montbrun / Passant de quelque nation / que tu sois / Respecte ses cendres / Ce sont les restes d'un des plus Braves / Parmis tous les Braves du Monde, / Du Général Montbrun. / Le M. d'Empire, Duc de Danzig, / lui a érigé ce foible monument. / Sa mémoire est dans tous les coeurs / de la grande Armée. /

villagers withdraw behind their wooden shutters I set out on my return journey with some trepidation, pressing on as fast as I could through a copse I could not skirt. I breathed more freely and slackened my pace when I reached the battlefield again, but here, too, I encountered stray peasants picking up firearms and discharging them at random. I gave them as wide a berth as possible and reached the safety of our billets in Elina by nightfall.

My report on my mission caused the commandant to abandon his idea of transferring the hospital to that particular village. He decided instead and as a first step to evacuate the seriously wounded and the sick back to Gzhaisk, following with the rest of his staff and the lightly injured as soon as suitable quarters became available.

Once again, I was entrusted with the task of seeing to both these enterprises. If I had regarded my first mission as no more than a nuisance I considered this second one downright hazardous. But having proved myself fit to accomplish the one I could hardly refuse the other. So I set out at daybreak, accompanied once again by my trooper. Along the main road, every now and again, we met groups of soldiers on their way back to their units after discharge from hospital. They never failed to express their surprise at seeing two solitary men venturing so far alone. At a French staging post, consisting of a few houses surrounded by a stockade to protect it against raiders, we were told that the road to Gzhaisk was extremely dangerous and that not a day passed without soldiers travelling along it singly or in pairs being attacked and murdered. I was advised to break my journey for the night at the next village, about three hours' ride away, and not to try to pass through the forest beyond in darkness. We reached the village at nightfall and found there some 100

French soldiers who welcomed every armed and able-bodied newcomer to their ranks as a reinforcement. At about eight o'clock at night we were joined by a number of refugees who said that a transport of Polish sick and wounded travelling from Mozhaisk had just been waylaid by a band of peasants between the staging post and the village—on the very stretch of road we had just travelled, in fact—and most of them had been killed. The news did nothing to allay our apprehensions, but in the pitch darkness there was nothing to be done but to stay where we were and on the alert. The night, however, passed without further incident.

The following morning my trooper and I continued on our way, passed through the wood—a journey of three hours—unmolested and got safely to Gzhaisk where my compatriots expressed the most lively surprise at our good fortune. With the help of the local hospital commandant I soon discovered a number of suitable houses, and on the following afternoon the first transport of sick and wounded, accompanied by a strong escort, arrived safely and without having met any trouble along the way. To complete my mission I should have returned next day by the same dangerous road but changed my plans on the specific orders of the commander of a newly arrived infantry battalion of convalescents, who refused to let me go to what he considered my certain death. Instead, I joined this battalion when it set out on its way to Moscow, travelling initially by a side road. On the 10th we re-joined the main highway and in Mozhaisk met the remainder of the Elina hospital which was now also trying to reach the Capital instead of retiring towards Gzhaisk. Much to my regret I was ordered to re-join the hospital at this point. On the 16th we reached Perkuzkovo, six hours' ride from Moscow, where we received instructions to turn

back and establish a hospital in Viazma or Smolensk, the Grand
Army having abandoned Moscow.* The infantry battalion,
however, continued on its way not withstanding, but I, despite
my pleas, was not allowed to accompany it and so never had the
privilege of seeing the ancient Capital of the Tsars.

Dejectedly I started out on the return journey. Our pace was
leisurely but the journey, because of the many ravines, none the
less exhausting. Near Mozhaisk the appearance of peasant Cossacks caused an alert. When we reached the big monastery near
the battlefield its occupants had just beaten off an attack by
them. I was in command of the rearguard and was stuck with a
large number of wagons in a ravine. Had they aimed their
attack at us they would at the very least have captured all our
wagons. The next day they murdered a courier and a French
trooper who had ridden ahead when we were no more than a
quarter of an hour away from the French staging post. From
this staging post onward until we reached Gzhaisk we had them
swarming around us constantly, and officers or men on their
own, even if they strayed no more than a hundred yards from
the main body, paid for their carelessness with their lives.

We reached Gzhaisk on 26th October, and Viazma on the
30th. That day we mourned the loss of two French adjutants,
good men both, who were cruelly done to death by peasant Cossacks quite near our convoy before we could come to their res-
cue. Between Semljewo and Dogorobuzh, on 3rd November, the
first fugitives of the Grand Army caught up with us, bringing
news of its retreat and incipient dissolution. On the 5th we
arrived at Dogorobuzh. By then, many fugitives had caught up
with and overtaken us, and by the end of the day we were in the

* Napoleon left Moscow on 19th October. Plans for the departure had, of
course, been made some time in advance.

very thick of the great retreat. The sick were accommodated here as well as circumstances permitted, and so my hospital service came to an end. On the 9th we reached Smolensk.*

When we began our retreat practically at the gates of Moscow our detachment had consisted of no more than 100 men, including some 50 who were fit for duty. Day by day this column grew, for whoever travelled along that road alone sought safety in attaching himself to our contingent whose defensive strength increased proportionately. In a matter of days we found ourselves in the company of generals and officers of every other rank, and every arm of the service was represented. Few were fully equipped, some carried an odd assortment of weapons, most were unarmed, but all, without exception, were burdened with a rich collection of loot, ranging from worthless rags to finest shawls, from tattered sheepskins to costly furs, from rickety carts to gilded coaches. The better armed soldiers and the least burdened with loot invariably also proved the most robust. For the rest, certain distinctions still prevailed. The infantry-man still travelled on foot, the trooper either rode a peasant pony or shared some kind of vehicle with several others, or at least drove before him, as long as it could stand upright, his galled nag loaded with his weapons. The confusion of nationalities paralleled that of services. Apart from Frenchmen there were Spaniards, Portuguese, Germans, Poles, Dalmatians, Illyrians, etc, etc. The march became increasingly arduous, provisions increasingly scarce.

The weather also played its part in the debacle. As early as the end of August it had begun to deteriorate. Though the days

---

* The same day as Napoleon, but by a different route. By taking the northern road he missed the battle of Malojaroslavetz, in which Kutusov barred Napoleon's way to the more southerly and less devastated regions of Russia.

were still warm the nights were getting cooler. With the beginning of September they grew distinctly chilly. Until 7th November, the skies had remained clear and blue, and the winds no rougher than they are in Germany at this time of year. But on the 8th winter suddenly set in.* A piercing northeasterly gale brought blizzards and a snap of frost which turned so bitter that by next day the cold had become all but unbearable. This continued until 12th November, when the weather became somewhat milder. Under the heavy traffic of carts and wagons the roads had begun to deteriorate even during the summer. With the frost and snow they improved somewhat, but the endless columns of marching soldiers, horses and vehicles of every kind soon made them so slippery that those on foot could move only with great effort, those on horseback were hard put to it to negotiate successive ravines, and thousands of vehicles had to be abandoned in the gulleys from which the weakened and unshod horses could no longer pull them. As for food, I, personally, had so far always found ways of getting it from the supply wagons. But now these supplies were exhausted, and henceforth I had to subsist on what I could occasionally buy at exorbitant prices. Famished and half frozen I reached Smolensk, without linen or warm clothing of any kind. My servant, hearing from some soldiers that I had been seized and murdered by partisans in the big forest near Gzhaisk, had taken my two horses and entire baggage with him and joined a convoy of wounded with which he retreated towards the Berezina.

* It has sometimes been suggested that an exceptionally early and severe winter created havoc with the Grand Army. On the contrary, winter set in rather late in 1812 and was not unusually severe by Russian standards.

IX

I N Smolensk I met several officers of my old regiment, which
had been dissolved after the Grand Army's retreat from Moscow, and with them I joined forces. We had found a common
billet in an empty house, heating the place with furniture and
woodwork from neighbouring, unoccupied houses. But for food
we had to pay almost its weight in gold. Apart from hunger, our
main preoccupation was our next move. No shelter could be
found for our horses. Some of them perished from the cold while
others were stolen at night, which in turn led to reprisals by our
troopers. I myself had already lost two of the four horses I had.
At Viazma I had found a serviceable, ownerless carriage to
which I had harnessed my horses. But I had been forced to
abandon it when we were still three days away from Smolensk,
the horses lacking the strength to haul it farther and the general
chaos of the retreating army making further progress with it impossible in any case. For four days we held out in Smolensk, stiff
with cold, determined not to leave the city before the Emperor
did so. We believed that our best chance of keeping on the move
was to be among the troops he selected for his escort. If this reduced, for the moment, our chances of getting enough to eat we
were quite prepared to put up with it and go on eating horse
flesh.

The city of Smolensk by now was little more than a heap of
rubble for no night passed without several houses going up in
flames. Not a single local inhabitant was left; all had turned
their backs on their homes and fled. The city, incidentally, built
as it is partly on the brow of a hill overlooking the Dnieper and
partly on its slopes, is sited quite romantically, and on the other
side of the river similar heights are attractively dotted with
houses and fretted by deep gulleys.

We had been told that in Smolensk we would find provisions

in plenty and, what we needed just as urgently, a corps of 40,000 fresh troops. We were to be cruelly disappointed. There was not so much as a single seasoned regiment, the city being inhabited entirely by the flotsam of the Grand Army.

Our hopes of joining the Emperor's escort came to nothing, but because of the cold we delayed our departure from Smolensk as long as possible. At last, on 13th November,* the day after the departure of the Imperial Guard, we, too, resumed our retreat. The first day's march passed without mishap. On the second we were less fortunate. Great swarms of Cossacks kept pace with the vast and motley column on both sides of the road, using every opportunity the terrain afforded to harry us with cannon fire and to wear us down with sporadic attacks. In Krasnoye we caught up with the imperial headquarters which, on the night from the 15th to the 16th, came under fierce but not very successful attack, † while we bivouacked half an hour away at Sarokino, anxiously awaiting the outcome of the battle. On the 16th and 17th we passed through Liady and Dubrovno, crossing the Dnieper and reaching Orzha on the 18th. After a day of rest we took the road to Minsk, constantly harassed by Cossacks, and reaching Bobr on the 22nd, where we were allowed another day of rest. Three more days of marching led us through Borisov, where we left the Minsk road and turned due east towards Vilna, and the banks of the Berezina. In a hamlet half an hour's ride from the river‡ we established our billets.

---

* A mistake in the date. Napoleon did not leave Smolensk until the 14th.

† This engagement, before Krasnoye, was a confused but quite serious affair in which the Russians, had they shown greater determination, might well have captured Napoleon.

‡ Probably the village of Studzianka or Veselovo, near where the crossing of the Berezina took place.

Here the remnants of the army drifted past us along the road, each man at his own pace and pleasure. Some abandoned the road for byways in the hope of finding something to eat. A few were lucky, but most paid for their foolhardiness with their lives or at least their liberty.

Near Krasnoye we had overtaken what remained of the army's disciplined core. In Orzha and again in Bobr we rejoined the rabble. As we approached the Berezina the disorganized throng began to crowd together. The regiments that remained intact were involved in constant skirmishes. Hour by hour the rearguard was trying to fend off the Russians pressing close behind. The number of battle-worthy units diminished day by day. We had hoped that our retreat could be halted at Minsk, but before ever we reached the city it had been seized by Admiral Chichagov, cutting off our line of withdrawal and forcing us to veer towards Vilna. On this town our remaining hopes were now centred.

I myself, from Smolensk onward, had been beset by every conceivable danger, hardship and privation. Constantly exposed on the march to enemy shot and shell, once barely escaping capture, in Orzha on the point of being roasted alive in a burning house and the previous day almost drowning in the Dnieper. I left Smolensk reasonably well mounted, all things considered, but by the 16th, in Liady, I had lost my useful little Cossack pony from weakness. My companions, more fortunate with their mounts, parted company with me and I continued on my way alone. At Orzha I had the good fortune to find a pair of top boots, laced, but on the very next day my last horse, a pony carrying my equipment, my top coat and my provisions, was captured together with my temporary servant. It had been everal days since this horse was last able to carry me. Now I had lost my best protection against the cold—my coat. Though a Württemberg officer, who did not know me but thought I had an honest face, gave me a loan, first of two ducats, and later of six from his regimental war chest, gold was a poor substitute for food, and of no use whatever against the cold.

On the 24th I was entrusted with the odd and, under the prevailing conditions, preposterous mission of assembling all the stray chasseurs wandering along the road and re-forming them into a fighting unit. Being on foot I had some success by day in gathering and keeping together a few of them, but as soon as night fell and we had to look for sleeping quarters they discovered that I had not so much as a bite of food or anything else to offer them. So away they melted again. Though I realized that I would receive a reprimand if I should happen to meet my commanding officer next day without my retinue, I neither could nor would make even an attempt to force these famished men to stay with me by putting them under formal orders.

The night of the 24th to the 25th I found a barn filled with hay into which I dug myself deep to escape the cold. The next night I spent in a wood, out in the open in the snow, without so much as a fire, and had I not pulled myself together every now and again to walk up and down and keep my circulation going I would undoubtedly have frozen to death. Next day, however, fortune smiled on me, for I met a Frenchman encumbered with two sheepskin coats, one of which he sold me for three ducats. This happy accident revived my spirits and I continued on my way more purposefully. The day after I was even luckier, for as I approached a small village I came upon a Württemberg officer who gladdened me with the splendid news that my servant with my baggage and two horses had just arrived there and was enquiring after me. I hastened on and found that the officer had spoken no less than the truth. I doubt if I ever had a more welcome surprise or felt greater relief and contentment in all my life. Now at last I had some decent clothes to wear and was well mounted once more. From now on I could face the cold in comparative comfort. Though hungry, I set out warmer and in better spirits than for a long time, and at nightfall reached a village where I found, in one house, a sergeant and fifteen chasseurs of my regiment—well mounted, well armed, who had come this far by side roads and had just re-joined the main highway. They had pork meat and honey in plenty, and looked upon me as an honoured guest. I needed no urging and without further ado seized the proffered meat and finally ate my fill—something I had not done for at least four weeks. But this reckless meal of pork, washed down with cold water, was followed by a bout of diarrhoea that plagued me for more than a year before I was completely cured.

Undoubtedly I would have done better to keep to starvation rations. Even as I ate I was uneasily aware that I should have to pay for my excess, but I never imagined that the consequences would be quite so disastrous. Yet such was my famished state that I doubt whether even the foreknowledge of such an outcome—indeed the certainty of imminent death itself—would have held me back from eating till I could eat no more.

When I left Smolensk I had provisions for no more than one day, that is to say, a small bag of flour. By the next day I was already reduced to eating horse flesh and though, from time to time, I did come upon something more palatable it was usually no more than scraps offered me out of kindness by people who had little enough to spare. Never was it enough to still the pangs of hunger. Even of the revolting horse flesh there was never enough to go round. In these circumstances nothing was more natural than the greed with which I fell upon the pork.

The weather had been very changeable during our march from Smolensk to the Berezina. When we left the city the cold was still bitter, but by evening milder weather had set in and by next morning it was thawing. The thaw, accompanied by fierce gales, lasted several days. But as soon as the wind dropped and the sky cleared the cold returned, though not as severe as at Smolensk. Twenty-four hours later the temperature rose again and from then onward until we reached the Berezina remained tolerable.

Roads and footpaths were generally very slippery and made walking or marching something of a penance. The many ravines exhausted the horses' strength as much as the treacherous surface which after the thaw turned to solid ice. On the whole, however, the terrain was less difficult than on the road from Dogorobuzh to Smolensk. In the small towns along our way some of the inhabitants had remained. Most of them were Jews who did a roaring trade with the sale of inferior provisions in exchange for the loot the troops found too burdensome to carry. The Christians, less adept at trade but more venturesome, mostly roamed the countryside, taking revenge on their wretched enemies by robbing and murdering the stragglers among them.

X

IN our hamlet half an hour's ride from the Berezina my chasseurs and I awaited our turn to cross the river, which we expected to come next morning. On the Emperor's orders two bridges had been thrown across the river near the village of Zembin, about fifteen miles above Borisov, a position which had first to be wrested from Admiral Chichagov in bitter fighting with heavy losses on both sides.* One bridge was intended for wagons and heavy equipment, the other for cavalry and infantry. By 27th November both were ready, but fate decreed that only a few were to have the chance of availing themselves of this safe and easy passage. On that day the bulk of the army, hard pressed by the pursuing Russians, was already massing on the banks of the river. But it was not until one o'clock in the morning of the 28th that the crossing began,† with men and vehicles now crowding in upon the bridges. That for the wagons soon collapsed under the strain, and though it was repeatedly mended had become quite impassable by midday. No engineers could be found to undertake further repairs, everyone was

* The crossing of the Berezina by the tattered remnants of the Grand Army, with a large enemy force lying in wait on the far side, was in fact a most extraordinary feat of arms. Napoleon took personal charge of the operation and by contrast with the chaos in its later stages, which Vossler describes, the first troops crossed in perfect order under the Emperor's eyes. French losses at the Berezina amounted to not less than 20,000 men, or about half the number that had reached the river under arms. In addition, a similar number of stragglers, including many women and children, were captured or perished.

† The bridges, in fact, were ready on the 26th, and the Old Guard crossed on the 27th. But the confusion and disarray caused by the host of stragglers led to endless delays. Vossler, waiting in his hamlet, was plainly not aware of these developments.

intent only on saving his own skin. An immense flood of men, horses and wagons now surged towards the other bridge. In the frightful crush men and horses were squeezed and trampled underfoot in their hundreds. The bridge was so narrow that it could only take two or three men abreast. Those lucky enough to reach it pressed on eagerly, but still not fast enough for those behind. At the approaches to the bridge, officers and orderlies tried to maintain some sort of discipline, but they were powerless in the face of the ever increasing pressure. On the bridge itself those who did not move fast enough were pushed over the side. Many waded into the water and tried to get on to the bridge that way, only to find themselves thrust back with sword and bayonet, most of them losing their lives in the attempt. Around one o'clock the cry went up 'the Cossacks are coming'. Those on the periphery knew they would be their first victims. Any speeding up of the movement towards the bridge seemed utterly impossible, but the cry electrified the rabble and spurred everybody to a final effort. Groups of cavalrymen closed ranks and ruthlessly rode down everything in their path. At the approaches to the bridge all semblance of order had ceased. Officers and orderlies had either fled before the raging mob or, if they stood their ground, had been cut to pieces. By now there were many trying to swim the river, but few succeeded. Most perished in the icy water. The fight for a passage reached its ultimate horror when the Russian guns began to find the range of the milling mass, spreading death and destruction. From now on it was a fight of each man against his neighbour. The stronger trampled their weaker comrades to the ground and struggled on until they, in turn, found their match in others stronger still. This ghastly scene ended only with the approach of darkness, when a detachment of French engineers on the far bank

F

dismantled their end of the bridge, leaving what remained behind—men, horses, guns and wagons of every description—at the Russians' mercy.

This day, and the cruel spectacle of it all, is something I shall never forget as long as I live. Not indeed, that I had an easy time of it myself. With my chasseurs I had set out towards the bridge at three o'clock in the morning. Even at that early hour we found ourselves preceded by an immense mass of humanity. An even greater one pressed on us from behind. Soon I had lost sight of my chasseurs in the crowd. Only my servant and Regimental Quartermaster Veikelmann were still with me. The crush became so intolerable that I would gladly have turned back had it been possible. Towards noon there came a great push from behind and from one side. Many men and horses were thrown to the ground, I among them. I was pinned under my horse, began to be trampled underfoot and resigned myself to the end when the quartermaster, with an immense effort, dragged me clear. Together we succeeded in getting my horse to its feet as well. I remounted and we continued to press on. But it was not long before I got separated from my servant and the quartermaster and finally lost sight of them. Then the warning of the Cossacks' approach arose and spread panic. Despairing of ever reaching the bridge I turned towards the river bank in the hope of getting on to it from there, even if it meant abandoning my horse. But presently I was thrown to the ground once more by a sudden sharp thrust of the mob, caused by the impetus of a group of well-mounted officers, and was severely trampled and bruised. Once more I was about to resign myself to my fate, seeing how remote, in these conditions, was the chance of a helping hand, when I saw looming above me a fellow-German, a Saxon cuirassier. I called out to him, he seized me by the arm, pulled me up and heaved my horse to its feet also. I found it hard to express my relief and gratitude. My plan of making for the river bank and reaching the bridge from there appealed to him. With his huge, powerful horse he pressed ruthlessly on, riding down whatever could not get out of his way in time, and I followed in his wake. By an almost superhuman effort we reached the bank. Here there were no mounted men and only a few on foot, we being among the first to try this desperate expedient. We found ourselves right beside the bridge. Quickly I dismounted and pulled myself up on to it, but was just as quickly pushed off again. The second attempt succeeded. A few sharp blows from the flat of the cuirassier's sword brought my horse leaping up on to the bridge beside me, and leading it at a smart trot I reached the far bank. There I waited for my servant, the quartermaster and the admirable cuirassier. The two former, to my great delight, soon joined me, but there was no sign of the cuirassier. Finally, when the Russian gunfire began to straddle the river and reach our bank, when the French engineers dismantled the bridge and all who had got safely across were gone, I, too, departed with a heavy heart. I never saw the cuirassier again.

A large part of the army, and all its equipment except for a few guns, were lost at the Berezina. Though most of what remained consisted of sick, wounded, worn-out soldiers without weapons, a few weeks' rest and care could have restored most of them and turned them once more into a formidable army. All who reached the western bank were glad to turn their backs on this ill-fated river and made haste to Vilna. But on the very night following the crossing the skies cleared and a frost set in which grew daily more severe until it reached a degree unheard-of even in these parts. Our road lead through Zembin,

Radescowiczi, Molodeczno, Smorgonye and Osmyany. All these places had been furnished with garrisons and stores of every kind, but with the news of the disaster that had overtaken us and of the approach of the Russian Army of the South, the former had been pulled back and the latter removed or destroyed. Nowhere did we find provisions, and the few inhabitants who had returned to their homes were as badly off as we.

After our crossing of the Berezina the Russians pursued us less hotly, for they, too, suffered badly from the awful cold. The remnants of our army withdrew as quickly as cold, hunger and exhaustion allowed towards Vilna, harassed less by the enemy than by indescribable misery and hardship. Those who travelled singly hastened ahead of the main army to seize what little food there was. Many fugitives had reached Vilna as early as 6th December, and in the two days that followed the influx was such that it had needed only a river ahead and the Russians behind to reproduce at the gates of the city the scenes of the Berezina crossing. Indeed, on the 9th they *were* re-enacted when the Russian spearhead reached the gates simultaneously with our rearguard and entered Vilna with them, pillaging and murdering as they went.* A goodly number of those who had been lucky enough to reach the western bank of the Berezina perished from the cold before ever they reached Vilna. Even the strongest constitutions succumbed where there was no protection from the climate. Every day I thanked my Maker that in the very nick of time he had provided me with what was, under the circum-

---

* Vilna was, in fact, bulging with provisions for the army. But because of lack of organization hardly any of them could be distributed before it was forced to abandon the city ahead of the pursuing Russians.

stances, the most precious possible gift: a fur coat. With Quartermaster Veikelmann and my servant I travelled as far each day as our horses would carry us. Despite our overcoats and furs we suffered pitifully from the cold, and eager though we were to press on we never passed a wayside fire or a burning house without warming ourselves at the flames. In this way we succeeded in keeping up both our spirits and our circulation. Thanks also to the good progress we made we managed to find almost everywhere enough provisions to feed the three of us. My diarrhoea, however, grew ever more violent and greatly sapped my strength. Soon I was incapable of mounting my horse unaided. I therefore resolved to stay in Vilna if ever I got there.

In Radescowiczi we met a Württemberg lieutenant with a detachment of lancers. He was waiting for the rest of his regiment. Two days later he got caught up in the rearguard and the following night froze to death with most of his men while on picket duty. Two newly arrived Neapolitan cavalry regiments, fresh and unscarred by battle, fared little better. We met them two days' march from Vilna, but three days later they were utterly demoralized by the cold and more than half of them had perished.* A detachment of some 2,000 Russian foot soldiers captured by the French in the battle for the Berezina crossings and driven with the army towards Vilna suffered a similar fate. Only a handful reached their destination. Most of them froze to death in bivouacs at night and many of the remainder, unable to keep up because of exhaustion or frost-bite, were shot by their

---

* According to Ségur, 600 Neapolitans of the Royal Guard came out from Vilna to take over the duty of escorting the Emperor and perished to the last man between Smorgonye and Vilna from the cold.

guards and left lying by the roadside. On 7th December Quartermaster Veikelmann and I reached Vilna. My servant had died from exhaustion in the little village where we had spent the previous night.*

* The previous day, December 6th, Napoleon had left the remnants of his army at Smorgonye to return to Paris alone. He put the unfortunate Marshal Murat in charge who led the remains of the Grand Army to final destruction before abandoning them to flee to his kingdom of Naples.

XI

IN Vilna I and a number of other Württembergers found billets in a house where we were protected at least from the worst of the cold. We shared it with its owners, who were all still living there. There was no shortage of food. We were given an advance of pay from the Württemberg war chest and the officers forgathered every day at the Lichtenstein café. I equipped myself with a fur hat, fur gloves and fur boots, regained some of my strength and gave up the idea of staying in Vilna. My two horses had also somewhat recovered. We cavalry officers gathered around General Count Norman and decided to continue our retreat from Russia under his leadership. Once we had put the river Niemen behind us it was agreed that each should make his own way home. In view of the great difficulties we were likely to encounter if we travelled by the main road General Norman decided, with our concurrence, to proceed along minor roads to Olitta, and for this purpose had engaged a Jew to be our guide. So as to avoid the great mass of fugitives, we delayed our departure from Vilna as long as possible and left the town only on 9th December in the morning—not much more than a couple of hours before the Russians entered it.

For most of the time we made our way through forests along makeshift roads dotted with a few lonely villages whose inhabitants had all stayed at home and provided us with food. We made two night stops and at noon on the third day reached the small town of Olitta, on the banks of the Niemen, without incident. Here we fortified ourselves with a tumbler-full of vodka and then proceeded to a safe and dignified crossing of the frozen river with feelings of the deepest gratitude for our deliverance. Who would have thought, only a few months back, when with hopes and spirits high we crossed the Niemen in the opposite direction, that our expedition would come to so lamentable an end! But perhaps it was just as well that we had no inkling of it, for who, knowing what miseries and hardships lay ahead, would have had the courage to advance?

On the west bank of the Niemen, in the Duchy of Warsaw, there lies at this point a small village which would have offered us very tolerable quarters, but heedless of the cold and of our weakened state we pressed on with the aim of leaving the ill-fated river, the origin of all our sufferings, as far behind us as possible. We reached Lieziskelli before nightfall and on the following two days passed through Simnas and Kalvariya, where we parted company and each of us took the road that was most likely to see him safely and quickly home.

The rest of my homeward journey concerns the travels of an individual, no longer connected with the Grand Army, of which I have no more to tell. So this, perhaps, is an appropriate moment to cast a look back on our retreat from Moscow and to set it in perspective. In doing this I shall try to confine myself strictly to what I personally saw, heard and experienced, relying as little as possible on the accounts of other witnesses, however trustworthy.

The retreat began with the Emperor's departure from Moscow. This was the signal for the general dissolution of the army. Many regiments were decimated, the cavalry, artillery and train had lost most of their horses. The stores were empty and each man was left to fend for himself. In theory, the army ought to have regained much of its strength by the time it left Moscow, for many sick and wounded had recovered in the interval and returned to their units. In fact, however, its stay in the Russian capital had greatly weakened it. A few minor skirmishes, mostly ending in equally minor defeats, were enough to produce a general rout. At Dorogobuzh we were joined by the first trickle of retreating soldiers. They had all been in Moscow where they had spent their time looting and whence they brought with them whatever they could carry. We were amazed at their appearance. Many carried no weapons, others were armed after a fashion, but their muskets were either unserviceable or they had run out of ammunition. These men were no longer soldiers but marauders and camp-followers, utterly undisciplined, bedizened occasionally with odd pieces of equipment but mostly burdened with bales of wool, linen, silk of every colour and description, with men's and women's furs from sable to sheepskin, hats and caps of every shape and size, fashionable boots and shoes, kitchen ware of copper, brass and iron, cutlery of silver and tin, pewter plates and dishes, glasses, goblets, scissors, needles, thread, waxed twine, and so on and so forth; in short, with every kind of object which the well-equipped peacetime traveller, on horseback or on foot, whether gentleman, journeyman, merchant, artist or whatever, could possibly require. Some travelled on foot and had already jettisoned much of their loot. Most were mounted, usually on wretched little Russian ponies, others on carts, barouches, diligences and coaches of every variety, including state carriages. There were common soldiers who had hired a retinue of others for their own and their horses' care and for the handling of as many as four carriages in their train. This was the spectacle which the first trickle of the retreating army presented. Their number swelled rapidly from day to day. With this motley crew who had joined our detachment for their own and their booty's greater safety we continued on our way. All discipline had broken down. At the appearance of the enemy the rabble huddled close together like sheep at the approach of the wolf, leaving their defence to us and to others who had not yet lost all sense of honour and decency. Yet the moment the danger was past they were once more the boldest and noisiest, and if there were any provisions about it was they who always somehow managed to spirit them away from their protectors. The longer the retreat lasted, the greater the number of units that lost their cohesion and swelled this miserable throng. Every day large numbers of them fell by the wayside, foundering under the weight of their spoils and falling into the hands of the pursuing Russians. Others, more sensibly, threw away their loot in time, abandoned coaches and carriages and tried to equip themselves with weapons. Hardly any of them had thought of providing themselves with food. Their minds were preoccupied only with money and money's worth, and consequently they found it increasingly difficult to support themselves the farther they went. Many lived on sugar, and when that was exhausted, on horsemeat and the meat of dead and even rotting cattle. In one village I saw Frenchmen digging carcasses of cattle, presumably diseased, from a hole in the ground, roasting them over a fire and devouring the meat with relish.

All these tribulations were greatly aggravated by the frost which set in on 8th November. Now the bundles of looted clothing were unwrapped and our column began to resemble a masquerade. The road was covered with ice. Precariously, those on foot staggered along the slippery surface. Painfully, the horses, their shoes long since shed, teetered under their heavy burden. In every ravine utter confusion developed. Carts and carriages by the hundred became hopelessly entangled, every driver tried to cut ahead of the next, no one wanted to be last, the wretched horses were cruelly maltreated. If they managed to breast one, two, or even three gulleys, sooner or later they would get stuck and become incapable of dragging their loads any farther. Then the carriages, which now were nothing but an obstacle and an encumbrance, were overturned, smashed up and burnt, their contents looted and dispersed. If it was artillery the horses had been drawing, the guns were spiked and dumped in a stream where possible, but often simply abandoned where they stood. Troopers drove their ponies, festooned with variegated loot, before them until they could go no farther and dropped in their tracks, whereupon they provided their masters with a last service: a meal of horseflesh. Those who felt their strength failing tried to reach a fire or a house, and when they had recovered somewhat and felt able to continue, set fire to the house in order to warm themselves thoroughly before setting off. If they did not do it, those that came after almost certainly would. Everybody tried to reach a village by nightfall, and the congestion in the dingy hovels was appalling. Yet many more were forced to spend the night in the open and these, partly to warm themselves and partly from envy of their more fortunate comrades, set fire to the houses in which the latter slept. On such occasions it even happened that those inside, for fear of the cold and out of stubbornness, refused to abandon their shelter and perished in the flames. News of such incidents spread quickly, with the result that the strongest banded together, drove the weaker out of the houses and mounted guard on the property against those they had evicted as if they were the enemy. In this way even the briefest occupancy of a house was frequently preceded by lengthy scuffles—as likely as not ending in someone's death. The weaker, compelled to spend the night in the open, gathered firewood, often breaking off parts of houses whose occupants had relaxed their vigilance, tore the thatch from the roofs and stole the horses and baggage of their comrades. But more often than not the weak did not even manage to reach the shelter of a village, falling by the wayside and freezing to death during the night. Even those fortunate enough to come upon an abandoned fire sometimes simply lay down beside it, too weak or tired to gather wood to keep it going. These, too, were usually found dead in the morning. Their corpses, frozen solid to the ground, were plundered by those that followed after, and used as seats at fires re-kindled with the chopped-up remains of their carts. Some, dragging themselves to a fire and craving for warmth, put their limbs right into the embers and perished, half roasted and half frozen to death.

The longer the retreat continued, the more ghastly became the sight of the fugitives. In the most frightful cold men could be seen toiling along the road without fur or overcoat, dressed only in a light suit, the frost visibly overpowering them. Their limbs gradually stiffened, they fell, picked themselves up painfully, staggered on a few paces, and fell once more never to rise again. Lack of sound and suitable footwear cost thousands their lives. Some showed their naked toes through torn shoes or boots, first purple, then frozen dark blue or brown, and finally black. Others had wrapped their feet in rags, scraps of leather, furs or skins, which preserved their toes provided they could find replacements when the original covering wore out. Of those who were lucky enough to survive, thousands lost hands, feet, noses and ears from the frost. In many cases extremities simply broke off, in others fingers and toes, and often whole arms and legs, had to be amputated.

The ravages of cold were equalled by those of hunger. No food was so rotten or disgusting as not to find someone to relish it. No fallen horse or cattle remained uneaten, no dog, no cat, no carrion, nor, indeed, the corpses of those that died of cold or hunger. It was not unknown even for men to gnaw at their own famished bodies. But not only men's bodies suffered unspeakably, their minds, too, became deeply affected by the combined assault of extreme cold and hunger. All human compassion vanished, each thought and cared only for himself and be damned to his comrade. With complete indifference he watched him lie down and die, without emotion he seated himself on his corpse by the fireside. Dull despair or raving madness had taken possession of many and they died muttering, with their last breath, the most horrible imprecations against God and man. Others became childish and perished as a result, though their physical strength might otherwise have carried them through. Yet others again fell into a torpor which prevented them from grasping the means of salvation when they presented themselves and thus they, too, stumbled to their deaths. All, without exception, had suffered some impairment, at least temporary, of their mental powers, which often manifested itself in a sort of dumb lethargy. The troops called it 'the Moscow Dumps'.

In closing this account of the retreat I would only add that I have by no means painted in excessively vivid colours, that in all things I have written nothing but the truth and that, as a matter of simple fact, I have never yet, to this day of writing in 1828, seen an account of the retreat that could be described as exaggerated. Indeed I am convinced that it would be impossible to exaggerate the misery endured by those that took part in it.

In view of all this, I think I need not emphasize further our delight at leaving the scene of our misfortunes and sufferings behind us and will now begin the story of my journey home to Württemberg.

XII

IN Kalvariya, on 13th December, I joined Lieutenant Count
Graevenitz and Lieutenant von Maucler in buying two sleighs
to which we harnessed our horses. Graevenitz and I occupied
one and Maucler, who was sick, the other with Quartermaster
Veikelmann. As coachman and servant we had engaged
Trooper Hoffmann, and the others Trooper Sommer. The cold
had somewhat abated during the preceding twenty-four hours,
though it was still bitter enough. On 14th December we left
Kalvariya and took the road to Goldap, lunched in Krovikresty
with a certain Count Pusinsky and got as far as Wysztitten by
nightfall. The following day we reached Goldap in East Prussia.
My friends * there welcomed us most warmly. Our account of
our adventures aroused their sincere sympathy and they did
everything in their power to help us forget our past sufferings.
But they, too, had suffered severely from the passage of the
French armies, at whose hands they had endured serious losses.
Us fellow Germans they treated as brothers, but their hatred of
the French, never entirely quenched since the events of 1807,
had taken on a new virulence. In Goldap we discarded our tattered and vermin-infested clothing and used the last of our funds
to buy new suits and clean linen. From Goldap we followed the
road by which our regiment had come, stopping wherever one
of us had been quartered on the outward journey and left agreeable memories on parting. Among the most notable of these
places were the small towns of Angersburg, Rastenburg and
Rössel. In all of them we found as warm a welcome as in Goldap
and in Rössel we took, as we had done in Goldap, a day of rest.
On 20th December we continued our journey in the direction

* Presumably the mayor, Alderman Reutter von Waldaukadel, with
whom Vossler had stayed while on detachment during the advance (see
Chapter IV).

of Danzig where the Württemberg contingent was to rendezvous. In Heilsberg we found good quarters with a merchant by
name of Romann, and the following day made the agreeable
acquaintance of the mayor of Wormditt and his wife. They advised us to be sure to take the road through Elbing to reach
Danzig. We followed their counsel and reached Elbing in the
late evening of 22nd December. The following day we discovered
that the Württemberg paymaster, Herdegen, was in town and
got from him, to our indescribable delight, a loan of 20
louis d'or from the Württemberg war chest together with the
news that the fortress of Thorn, on the Vistula, had been desig-
nated the Württemberg rendezvous instead of Danzig. Leaving
Elbing almost immediately we passed through Marienburg the
same day and reached Marienwerder on the evening of the 24th,
where we were billeted with Doctor Burkhardt, with whom we
spent Christmas. Our host's and his wife's boorishness, however,
did much to spoil the day for us and we were glad to leave them
on the 26th to continue our journey. After two days' drive, during which we passed through the town of Graudenz and caught
a glimpse of the fortress of the same name, we reached the
town and fortress of Thorn on the right bank of the Vistula on
28th December. But here, too, we stayed only briefly, for we had
no desire to endure the siege to which the fortress was likely soon
to be subjected, longing only for a return to our homes. We left
Thorn after a day of rest for the small town of Inowroclaw
in the Duchy of Warsaw, ten hours' march distant, where
the remnants of the Württemberg contingent were being assembled. All over East and West Prussia and the Duchy of Warsaw there remained traces of the passage of the French armies in
the spring and summer of the same year. They were most plainly
visible in East Prussia, and more especially in the northern part

of the province, for discipline had slackened progressively as the armies approached enemy territory and the start of the campaign. We found, accordingly, much misery in these parts and had no reason to be surprised at the hostile reception we sometimes experienced. Nevertheless it was usually those who had suffered worst who treated us most kindly, and on the whole I cannot praise the attitude and behaviour of the East Prussians enough. The same, unfortunately, cannot be said of the West Prussians, and here, with two exceptions—Wormditt and Graudenz—we generally met nothing but hatred and contempt openly expressed. In the Duchy of Warsaw we drew a distinction between the nobility and the common people. The former treated us kindly, but the latter loathed and shunned us.

The countryside between Goldap and Elbing is tolerably fertile, and very much so towards the river Nogat. It is generally flat and monotonous in appearance, with few points of eminence or interest. The lowlands of Elbing are regarded as one of the most fertile districts of Prussia. Around Graudenz the soil again turns sandy, degenerating into a veritable desert around Culmsen and Thorn. The architecture of East Prussia is similar to that of the Duchy of Warsaw, though somewhat cleaner and more gracious in appearance. The small towns of Heilsberg and Wormditt are old but not badly built. Elbing is a considerable, thriving and soundly constructed place. In the neighbourhood of this town the villages are more pleasing and prosperous. In the valleys of the Nogat and the Vistula, indeed, they surpass the finest and richest villages in Southern Germany. The walls and houses of Marienburg testify to the town's great age; Marienwerder, on the other hand, boasts many more new and elegant buildings. Graudenz is old but well built and seems to be fairly prosperous. The fortress near by stands on a small

eminence but neither fortifications nor houses are visible from the road. The place, we were told, has only very few building above ground as its only inhabitants, the garrison, live in casemates.

To the west of Graudenz, where the soil deteriorates yet again, the villages, too, are more poorly built, the rooms less comfortable and clean, reverting to typically Polish standards around Thorn. Thorn itself is a considerable and thriving town with sizeable industries. Its many streets are well paved, and some of its houses would grace a much larger city. The little town of Inowroclaw contains, besides many houses of the Polish type, quite a number of better buildings, all of them a legacy of Prussian rule. On the whole it can be counted among the better Polish towns.

This was the place where, according to the orders of our king (who had refused to credit reports of the army's total rout) the remnants of the Württemberg contingent were to be assembled and reorganized, and where they were to remain until the arrival of reinforcements and the start of a new campaign against the enemy. The generals, however, were well aware that no such orders could possibly be carried out. They had therefore chosen one of their number to travel to Württemberg and enlighten the King as to the true state of affairs and to persuade him, if possible, to recall what troops had been salvaged from the disaster. As a result, and to our very great satisfaction, we did not have to wait long for orders to the officers to make their own way home individually by the quickest route, and for the troops, under the command of a few officers, to be brought home as well by easy stages. This order reached us on 6th January 1813, and on the 7th I was on my way back to Württemberg.

During my stay in Inowroclaw, from the end of December

G

until 7th January, I was continually plagued by diarrhoea and stomach cramps. In the state of general debility in which I found myself medication brought no relief. I was among those officers who were to return home on their own. I therefore entrusted my two horses to the care of the depot commandant, with whom I had already left one while in Russia, drew some hundreds of guilders from the war chest, provided myself with what few clothes I needed and bought, in partnership with Lieutenant Count Graevenitz, a Polish pritschka for the journey. Trooper Hoffmann was to be our escort.

XIII

WITH the most joyful emotions we set out for home on the morning of 7th January. Though our pritschka lacked a hood it did provide enough room for us to sit or lie down inside as we pleased. Fresh horses, usually sturdy cobs, were available at every relay station. We took the road through Pakocz and Budewitz to Poznan, which we reached the following day. We stayed only a few hours and then resumed our journey, spending the night of the 9th in Fraustadt, our last stopping place in the Duchy of Warsaw. On the 10th we crossed the Oder, passed Glogau, where we lunched, and travelled through Sagan, Surau, Muskau, Hoyerswerda and Königsbrück, reaching Dresden, the Saxon capital, on the 12th. Here we rested for two days and then, on the 15th, drove down the Elbe valley to Meissen, across the Erz mountains through Freyberg, Chemnitz and Zwickau to Plauen in Voigtland, on through Hof and Bayreuth to Nüremberg where we arrived on the 18th, and on to Ansbach the next day. On the 20th we reached Ellwangen and took another day's rest. The following day saw us at Gmünd and the 23rd at Ludwigsburg, where the Governor informed us that all officers returning from Russia were allowed leave until the end of the month—all of seven days—during which they were at liberty to go wherever they liked within the Württemberg borders. So we carried straight on to Stuttgart.

Thus at last, after innumerable hardships and dangers, I was back in my own country. In a mere seventeen days we had covered a distance of more than 500 miles, and taken three days of rest in the process. We had traversed many countries and had met everywhere with a decent reception—varying, of course, according to circumstances, but never really bad.

Wherever we went we were gaped at like freaks, for we were among the few who had escaped the universal disaster. Every-

where we were made to give, over and over again, an account
of our own adventures, of the plight of the army and of the appalling hardships we had suffered. Yet such is human nature
that there were always some who felt our tale was not harrow-
ing enough and argued that we could not therefore have experienced the campaign and the retreat in its entirety. Nowhere did
we have any difficulty in obtaining bed and board—either at
inns or in private houses—though nowhere except in Dresden
did we tarry longer than our exhausted condition required. In
the Duchy of Warsaw we found less cause for complaint about
the quality of our billets than during the previous spring, partly
because we stopped only at relay stations and partly also, no
doubt, because our experiences in Russia had made us more
modest in our demands. In Poznan we stayed only a few hours,
to take a look at the town and to buy some clothes. Poznan and
Fraustadt are the largest and most solidly built towns we saw on
our journey through the Duchy of Warsaw from Inowroclaw.
Both have many handsome buildings and, like Kösten and Suy-
gel, are striking examples of the benefits the country derived
from Prussian administration. In fact, the nearer the traveller
approaches the Silesian frontier the more agreeably is he impressed by the level of prosperity and cleanliness of the inhabitants. The Poles grieved deeply to see us go, for the circumstances of our departure clearly indicated that the days of
French rule were drawing to a close—at any rate for the time
being if not for ever—and were likely to be replaced by sterner
and more oppressive government. Nevertheless they showed us
great kindness and gave us every assistance we could fairly expect of them—especially in Fraustadt.

The countryside between Inowroclaw and the Silesian frontier is flat, mainly sandy but not infertile, and the whole of this

region is among the most prosperous and attractive in the Duchy of Warsaw.

In Silesia we could not help noticing a certain secret satisfaction at the disaster that had overtaken the Grand Army, but on the whole people were too polite to gloat openly. Quite on the contrary, they treated us with much sympathy, though some were honest enough to say that this was because we were Germans rather than because of our connection with the French. Only in Glogau, despite—or, indeed perhaps because of—the presence of a French garrison, did we encounter open hostility. But for both our own sake and that of other fugitives yet to come we pretended to take the insults hurled at us as jokes or misunderstandings. In general we avoided, in our contacts with the local inhabitants, all political discussion and this restraint, no doubt, had a lot to do with our hosts' friendly behaviour. In Glogau, because of the incidents I mentioned, we were loath to stay longer than absolutely necessary, so I can say no more about the town's fortifications than that they appeared particularly strong on the side facing the Oder. The streets along which we passed were well paved but in part very narrow. The town bustles and the inhabitants seemed sprightly and merry. Several years of French occupation have evidently imbued them with a fierce hatred of the French. Near Neustädel we saw vineyards which brought poignant memories of our fatherland. Whereas the country around Glogau is flat, Neustädel lies among hills, and from there onward the vast plains are gradually absorbed in a more varied landscape until, near Hoyerswerda, the plain takes over once more. Sagan, the last small town in Silesia, is a pleasant little place. The whole region, from Glogau to Sagan, is fairly densely populated and intensively cultivated. The villages are neat and the houses reflect their owners' prosperity.

The first small Saxon town we reached was Surau. It is a well-built place but Muskau, our next stop, is even better, and beautifully situated. For this reason, and because of the courtesy of our hosts there, I have pleasant memories of it. Spremberg and Hoyerswerda are smaller places and relatively poor. Königsbrück, on the other hand, is a flourishing town.

Up to this point our many hosts, despite all their courtesy, had shown a certain constraint and reserve in their dealings with us, which we ascribed mainly to their fear of disease, and in particular of typhoid, which they suspected every refugee of carrying. They were also, no doubt, disgusted by the filthy condition in which many of the fugitives turned up. Even we, despite our repeated changes of clothing, were not yet entirely free from vermin. For this reason we decided when we got to Dresden to spend some time not only resting our weary carcasses and seeing the sights, but also to devote a good deal of care to the cleansing and disinfecting of our apparel.

A broad, handsome and elaborately carved stone bridge leads from the suburbs across the river Elbe into Dresden proper. We reached the city late in the evening and allowed ourselves the luxury of staying at our own expense in one of the city's best inns. On the two following days we went sight-seeing around the capital. It is a splendid city, the houses of stone, the streets not excessively wide, yet not narrow, either, and always spotlessly clean. In addition to the royal palace there are a number of other palatial buildings and several beautiful churches, among which the Frauenkirche, modelled on St Peter's cathedral in Rome, is outstanding. The view from the cupola of this church is vast and uniquely picturesque. There are a number of art collections of various kinds which are well worth seeing. Unfortunately the so-called 'Green Vault' with its incomparable picture gallery was closed. The Armoury contains a huge collection of weapons and suits of armour of every period, many of them extremely rare. In the store rooms of the Meissen porcelain factory a particularly beautiful dinner service intended for the French Emperor happened to be on display, as well as a great number of handsomely painted vases and other table ware. I would dearly have liked to buy some small item to take home as a souvenir, but I had to husband my resources. The Brüehl Palace is situated in the gardens of the same name, which are landscaped with perfect taste regardless of expense and afford a dazzling view on to the wide and handsome Elbe. The opera performance we attended was distinguished by excellent singing and charming stage sets.

Dresden is most romantically situated on the river Elbe with its busy riparian traffic and excels in grace, to my mind, all other royal residences in Germany. The inhabitants are good-natured, courteous and polished, much given to entertainments and diversions. They seemed as yet untouched by the dark future looming over Germany. At our inn we were very well served and fed, a circumstance accurately reflected in our bill.

We left Dresden as we had arrived—with post horses—our next stop being Meissen. The road runs along the right bank of the Elbe. I have never seen a richer or more beautiful landscape than this valley. It is flanked on either side by steep hills covered with enchanting orchards and vineyards. The valley itself is dotted with pretty villages and manor houses, the roads perfectly level and perfectly maintained, the local population well dressed, well fed and radiating contentment; all of which made the most agreeable impression on me and put me in an excellent humour. For four hours we travelled through this Saxon paradise.

Meissen's ancient castle is a landmark visible from afar. It is the family seat and one-time residence of the Markgraves of Meissen and lies on a lofty promontory of the Erz mountains. A covered bridge, part stone and part wood, leads across the Elbe into the small town, built into the mountain, charming at a distance and not badly constructed on closer inspection. The castle has been for many years now the home of the celebrated porcelain factory which obtains its clay from pits a day's journey distant. It charges high prices for its wares but excels all other similar products in Germany in beauty of workmanship, glaze and decoration. We inspected the entire factory with the greatest interest and each of us bought a small object by which to remember our visit.

From Meissen our way took us across the Erz mountains. Here Nature presents a sterner countenance. Whereas the Saxon plain-dweller lives comfortably off the fruits of the soil his mountain cousin, in his more austere environment, must earn his living laboriously by mining coal and by equally laborious work in the factories. Every town, every village, has a factory and the appearance of the inhabitants bears witness to the effect of this type of labour on their health. The complexion of the miner is as grey as his place of work. However, the region shows every sign of bustling activity, and trade and commerce flourish. As everywhere else in Saxony, the people here are courteous and hospitable.

The next small town we reached after Meissen was Stössen, distinguished only by a large and ancient castle. Freyberg, where we stayed the night, is a famous resort, quite sizeable, well built, but sparsely inhabited. It, too, boasts a large and handsome castle. There are several pits near this town, but much as we would have liked to we could not afford the time to inspect any of them. Chemnitz is an important and thriving commercial and industrial centre, with many handsome buildings. A little farther along the road you come to the village of Oberlungwitz, consisting of two rows of houses in a very narrow valley, stretching on either side of the road, for a quarter of an hour's drive. The small town of Lichtenstein with its castle is romantically situated. Zwickau, the last town before leaving the Saxon part of the Erz mountains, is a commercial centre of some importance and the home of several factories. It is a busy and thriving place.

Now we had reached the Voigtland, a region just as industrious and full of workshops as that we had just left and part, in fact, of the same mountain range. Reichenbach is a pretty little place, Plauen old, of no great importance, but with a large palace.

On the 17th we reached Bavaria. After Plauen, the courtesy and polish of the Saxons gradually gives way to the rougher manners of the Bavarians. In Hof, a sizeable town, the contrast is still mild, but no more than four hours farther along the road, in Münchberg, the traveller is made uncomfortably aware that he is in another country. Between Hof and Münchberg the peaks of the Fichtel mountains loom to the right, but then the countryside flattens out once more. In Bayreuth we found good billets at the sign of the Golden Anchor. We arrived there early enough to allow us to visit the theatre. The country around Bayreuth is dotted with many handsome villages. The town itself is well built and has a large population. Hilpoldstein is a shabby little place, but the castle near by, built on a high, solitary rock, gives the surroundings an element of romance. On the evening of the 18th we reached Nüremberg. We were lodged at the sign of the Imperial Eagle, where we found the host and his wife most obliging. Here, too, we spent the evening at the theatre, and afterwards in conversation with our host. The following morning we took some hours off to walk through the great, ancient and once so wealthy city, which seemed to have retained some of its prosperity even in our time. It lies in a plain, with mountains visible only in the distance. Ansbach, through which we passed next, is quite a pretty town with a large, handsome castle. Here we were quartered with State Secretary Schnitzlein and found him and his family kind and friendly. I took the opportunity of calling on a man by name of Scheuermann who formerly worked for my uncle Kinzelbach, whom I had known well when I attended Stuttgart high school, and who was surprised and delighted to see me.

On the 20th, at last, we were back on our native soil. At Ellenbach, the first Württemberg village we came to, we stopped outside the inn and drank a toast to our fatherland in home-grown wine. At Ellwangen we put in a day's rest. We could not have wished for a better reception. They all vied with each other in spoiling and cosseting us and took the greatest trouble to make us forget our past sufferings. On the 21st we continued on our way, but no farther than Schwäbisch Gmünd where we lodged with a merchant by name of Mayer and spent the evening at the inn according to approved Württemberg custom over a glass of wine. I need hardly point out that here, as almost everywhere else, we were the talk of the town and plied with questions into the small hours. Next day, as I have already told, we continued on to Stuttgart by way of Ludwigsburg.

So here I was, back home, pale and emaciated, my clothes in tatters, and penniless. I had lost my entire equipment, and of the ten horses I had owned at one time or another eight had perished. All I had to show for my pains were debts of about a hundred guilders. The journey from Inowroclaw to Stuttgart had almost completely exhausted my physical strength. My mental state, on the other hand, had greatly improved and I could fairly expect my physique to follow suit in time. But it would certainly need a prolonged period of rest. Though I still suffered from diarrhoea and a weak stomach, both had improved considerably and were likely to mend completely by and by. They did not, even then, prevent the gradual recovery of my general state of health.

On Sunday, 24th January, we paraded in Stuttgart before His Majesty the King, the Crown Prince and the general commanding the garrison. During the inspection a great many promotions were announced, including my own, though it was a modest one in all conscience. I was granted no more than the rank of a full lieutenant. After visiting a few relatives I left by special post at five o'clock in the evening for Tuttlingen, to be re-united with my mother and sisters. They received me with deep and heartfelt happiness, though they were much concerned at my appearance. I could not have been better cared for, and had I but been allowed to stay at home a while, my health would undoubtedly have recovered completely. During the five days I spent at Tuttlingen I was not only obliged constantly to repeat the tale of my adventures to family and friends, but also plied with questions from a stream of people from the town and surrounding countryside seeking news of relatives and acquaintances, of whom I could reassure only very few and had to send the great majority away uncomforted. Trooper Hoffmann, whom I had brought back with me to Tuttlingen as my servant, was the toast of every inn he visited—and there were few he left out—for the tales he could tell of the Russian campaign, and especially of the retreat from Moscow. On 30th

January I left Tuttlingen again and reached Ludwigsburg the next day. Throughout the land the Russian war and the retreat were the main topics of conversation, and wherever they went the returned warriors met with the sincerest sympathy. At their tales of wellnigh indescribable suffering every eye grew moist. There was no one who would have grudged us a longer period of rest as a reward for our privations, but alas, circumstances decreed otherwise.*

* These circumstances were Napoleon's 1813 campaign. Though Prussia had now joined Russia as his enemy, Bavaria, Württemberg and, for a time, Saxony, remained faithful. In an amazingly short space of time the Emperor had raised formidable new armies with which he set out to defeat the Alliance in central Germany.

PART TWO

ON 3rd February 1813 the regiment of mounted Duke Louis Chasseurs which, since October 1812, had existed in name only, was re-formed. In other words, it was newly equipped with officers, men and horses. The men had been conscripted during the month of January and the horses bought in Leipzig and brought to regimental headquarters by General von Fell. In common with every cavalry officer who had taken part in the Russian campaign I received a gift of one horse and twenty louis d'or with which to equip myself, and when the remnants of our regiment returned from Inowroclaw, bringing my two other horses with them, I was once again adequately mounted. That very same day we assembled in the garrison of Winnenthal where officers and men were lodged in the castle and its out-buildings. We lost no time and began drilling the men and training the horses on 4th February, continuing the process intensively over the next few weeks. By the end of the month we had advanced to troop and squadron exercises and by the end of March men and horses were fit for combat. As the regiment was gradually brought up to strength part of it was despatched to Waiblingen, and later no less than half of it to Esslingen where I also arrived during the first days of March with Major von Reinhard's squadron.

In Winnenthal my health was seriously undermined by recurrent bouts of typhoid, but the local doctor, Doctor Christmann, succeeded in keeping the attacks under control. My stay in Esslingen coincided with a period of freedom from the infection and allowed me to regain some of my strength.

By the end of March, then, we were ready to set forth, and in the first days of April the two squadrons were ordered to move to Winnenden to join the squadrons already stationed there for regimental exercises. We arrived on 6th April but the very next day received counter-orders assigning us to billets on the frontier, in the general direction of Würzburg. So we left Winnenden on the 8th and marched, via Hall and Langenburg, to the outskirts of Rothenburg on the Tauber, which we reached on the 12th and where we were billeted in some of the surrounding villages.

My Stuttgart relatives had come to Esslingen on 5th April to see me off, and I had taken leave of them with a heavy heart. I was filled with misgivings about my weakened body, barely recovered from renewed attacks of fever and now about to be exposed to further hardships. On the march from Winnenden to Rothenburg I was, in fact, carried along in a chaise behind the regiment and did not resume active service until 23rd April. The villagers along our route waved and cheered us on our way and many showed concern for me, so recently and painfully returned from Russia, so obviously unfit, and yet on my way once more to new battles. Yet I must admit that despite the frail state of my health I was happy enough to continue my military career, and expected the approaching spring to work wonders on my physique. Near Sülzbach the people served us with refreshments in the open fields amidst great merriment and good fellowship in which I joined as far as my infirmities allowed. In Hall, too, we were well received, and in the vicarage at Spielbach I spent most of my time in bed in order to regain my strength. In this I succeeded so well that from that time on I was able to abandon the chaise and continue the march on horseback.

II

WE left our billets near Rothenburg on 17th April. With two regiments of cavalry and three of infantry under the command of General von Franquemont we formed the 1st Württemberg Army Corps which was to join the French army in Saxony. Our route lay through Niederstetten, Weikersheim and Mergentheim towards Würzburg. In Mergentheim we joined the other regiments and took leave of our fatherland. On 20th April we skirted the splendidly situated fortress of Marienburg, crossed the Main, passed through the beautiful town of Würzburg and continued as far as the vicinity of Rottenburg where we had a day's rest before moving on in the direction of the Thuringian forest. Through Lauringen and past the Würzburg-owned fortress of Königshofen we reached Römhild in Saxony, a small town with an ancient palace, on the 25th. Next day we passed through Hildburghausen and Schleusingen, continuing our journey the day after through the Thuringian forest as far as Königsee. On the 29th we had our last day of rest in Heilsberg and the surrounding villages, and next day carried on via Rudolstadt, Jena, Camburg and Naumburg to the neighbourhood of Lützen, which we reached on the evening of 3rd May.

This was the starting point of our next campaign, but before I begin to tell of it I want to cast a backward glance at the countryside and the people we encountered on our march.

That part of Württemberg where we crossed the frontier of our homeland is among the most beautiful in the whole country. The valley of the Tauber river near Mergentheim is a sheer delight, with many spectacular views. The inhabitants are comfortably but not excessively well off, partly because their economy is based almost exclusively on viticulture and partly because by tradition and upbringing they are less hardworking

H

and thrifty in their habits than other Württemb ergers. Leaving
the Tauber valley and following the main road towards Würzburg the countryside declines in interest, though parts of it are
charming enough. But when, near the fortress of Marienthal, the
view opens on to Würzburg and the Main valley a scene is revealed of such grace and splendour as can hardly be matched
anywhere in Germany and certainly nowhere surpassed. The
city of Würzburg itself is large and populous, the streets elegant, the houses handsome. The palace is marvellously situated
near the river. Beyond Würzburg the countryside levels out and
there are no more vineyards. The people of the Main valley are
gay and vivacious—on the far side they show a graver and more
serious disposition. The constant billeting of troops in these
parts had left very visible traces. The fortress of Königshofen lies
in a wide plain and is of no great importance. Around Schleusingen the people were as hospitable as ever, but the fare they
had to offer had become plainer, for since our last visit they had
been compelled to entertain many uninvited guests. The same
condition applied to other parts of Saxony as we progressed.
The university town of Jena is a neat, prettily situated place and
in passing through its streets I recalled with amusement some of
the true and apocryphal tales told about its students which I
had heard at various times. I was treated to several more that
same evening by the merry vicar of Löbstadt. I was particularly
interested, however, in his description of the battle and battlefield of Jena of 14th October 1806* of which he had been, so to
speak, an eye-witness.

I would gladly have spent some time in the town of Naumburg, partly to investigate the bustling trade for which it is

---

* Where Napoleon inflicted a decisive defeat on Prussia and forced her to
sue for peace.

famed and partly to learn more about the Hussite wars* and the siege the town underwent in those days. But the business on which we were engaged brooked no such delay. Throughout our journey across Saxony we were constantly reminded that we were following in the footsteps of many armies in recent times and that any lack of hospitality we experienced was due not so much to ill-will on the part of the inhabitants as to the impoverished state to which they had been reduced. The town of Jena in particular was still labouring painfully under the damage it had suffered during the battle of 1806. The countryside in general is attractive, even if it lacks the charm of some parts of Southern Germany. Husbandry and cattle-breeding are the main props of the country's economy.

As early as 23rd April, when we were still on Würzburg territory, we had begun, partly by way of useful training for our inexperienced young officers and men, partly because enemy scouting parties had penetrated beyond the Thuringian forest, to send out nightly patrols and to mount guard on our bivouacs. At first this was regarded as a somewhat superfluous precaution but very soon it was justified by events. At dawn on 30th April there appeared ahead of our outposts a party of Cossacks who, on perceiving our precautions, fired a few shots and then made off in a hurry.

On 2nd May I had orders to find billets in Priessnitz and when I arrived there with a mere handful of men discovered that a score or so of Prussian hussars had only just left the place. Indeed, the inhabitants at first mistook us for another contingent of Prussians and were visibly disappointed when they discovered

* The burning at the stake, early in the fifteenth century, of the religious reformer John Huss led to serious disturbances in many parts of Southern and Central Germany.

their error. Near Naumburg we encountered many wounded who brought us news of the battle of Lützen and of the French victory there.* Not far beyond Naumburg we made contact with unidentified forces and prepared ourselves for our first battle before realizing, to our mutual relief, that they were French. That evening we reached the battlefield of Lützen, situated on a wide plain, and camped beside a village that had been burnt down during the battle. Dusk had already descended, so for that evening at any rate we were spared the sight of the carnage that had taken place there the previous day. During the night two wounded Prussian corporals were brought in who could give us a fuller account of the battle and who, moreover, left us in no doubt as to their disgust at Germans who were still fighting on the French side. It goes without saying that this did not in any way influence our treatment of them, and they were given every possible medical care for which they showed themselves duly grateful. Dawn revealed to us a ghastly sight of the bloody execution done so recently in this place. A great mass of corpses, some of them terribly maimed, weapons and equipment of every kind, smashed wagons and shattered guns littered the ground all around us, and many a young recruit no doubt wished himself safely back home beside his parents' hearth. For several hours we awaited orders to move on, and it almost seemed as if our commanders wanted to give the unseasoned troops a chance of accustoming themselves to their new profession.

At last, at ten o'clock in the morning of this, the 4th of May

* On 2nd May 1813 Napoleon outgeneralled and defeated a superior force of Russians and Prussians under General Wittgenstein at Lützen. His forces were too weak and inexperienced to allow him to exploit his victory and make it decisive.

we finally marched off across part of the battlefield and joined forces around noon near Pegau with the 4th French Army Corps under the command of General Bertrand, of which we formed part from then on. Leaving Leipzig on our left we turned in pursuit of Blücher's army towards the Erz mountains and camped the following night near the little town of Luckau. Next day our march took us through the richest region of Saxony around Altenburg as far as Rochlitz. All day long we had passed great masses of infantry and had a number of skirmishes with Prussian rearguards. The night of 6th to 7th May we camped near Taunberg and the following morning reached Mittelwayda in the foothills of the Erz mountains, where a general halt was called. After a few hours of rest my squadron advanced on to a small eminence on one side of the village with orders to flush the enemy from a copse to our front where they were ensconced. But before we could mount the attack they had melted away. So the army corps moved on through Haynichen to Reichenbach. There we received the news that Blücher had already withdrawn to the other side of the Elbe. This intelligence was confirmed by a sweep we undertook to the depth of two hours' ride, as far as Nossen. Apart from a few stragglers whom we took prisoner we made no contact with the enemy.

On 8th May, at Herzogenwalde, we joined the main French army but were almost immediately ordered to move on to Pirna where we were to secure the bank of the Elbe. We completed this operation by the morning of the 10th. The opposite bank was occupied by Russians, which meant that we had to keep a sharp look-out. Nevertheless the majority of our forces were quartered in billets. On the 11th we followed the course of the river downstream, passed through Dresden and crossed the Elbe, where the Emperor Napoleon stood to watch the crossing and to inspect the Corps as it passed by. We continued along the Königsbrück road as far as Lausitz through wooded country where we were persistently harried by enemy patrols and took Lausitz by storm at nine o'clock in the evening. On the 12th we advanced on Königsbrück, passed through the town and set up camp on the far side of the road to Bautzen, with my squadron right in the van. In the afternoon I made a reconnaissance along the Hoyerswerda road as far as Schmorka, an hour's ride from Königsbrück, without making any contact with the enemy. The following day another patrol went out to reconnoitre the same stretch of road. With ten of my troopers I, being already familiar with the terrain, was attached to this patrol which apart from us consisted of two companies of Croatian infantry and twenty Neapolitan lancers under the command of a Neapolitan squadron commander, Count Mirelli. Also attached to us were two French staff captains. Our orders were to push forward for two hours as far as Schwegnitz. If we still had made no contact with the enemy by then we were to gather information about his retreat and the strength of his forces which had passed along this road.

With my troopers I led the van of this expedition, the Croatians combing the woods bordering the road on either side from Schmorka as far as Schwegnitz and beyond. We encountered nothing of interest along the road except, on approaching Schwegnitz, two horsemen on the far side of the village who made off at full gallop towards the woods. We set off in pursuit but failed to catch them before they disappeared among the trees. The inhabitants of the village told us they were local peasants who had departed in such haste presumably for fear of losing their horses. We had no means of verifying these assertions and therefore thought it prudent to take all necessary

precautions. We consequently ringed the village with outposts
and concentrated the infantry at the entrance to the place. Our
commander, accompanied by me, the two French staff captains,
a Croatian captain and his lieutenant immediately proceeded to
the parsonage where the parson, the village headman and the
schoolmaster were closely questioned about the enemy, one of
the staff officers noting down their answers. The interrogation
lasted about an hour during which, as nothing seemed to stir
in the surrounding countryside, all the other Croatian officers
had gradually joined us at the parsonage. The interrogation was
almost complete when a Croat soldier entered hurriedly, drew
his captain aside and whispered something in his ear. Visibly
disturbed the latter turned to us and informed us that a number
of Prussian hussars had been seen in the woods. We immediately
left the parsonage and hastened to our detachments, gathering
them all together on a small hillock from which the entire village and its surroundings could be kept under observation.
From there we saw—not, indeed, Prussian hussars, but a large
force of Cossacks who burst from the woods on every side with
fierce war cries. Already our outposts were hurrying back towards the shelter of the village where we set out to join them.
But when we reached the main body of our detachment we
found that many of the soldiers had already broken ranks and
begun to disperse inside the village, and the remainder were on
the point of following their example. They paid no heed to the
orders of their officers who in their turn already seemed to have
given up all hope. In these circumstances the Neapolitan lancers, my troopers and I, if we were to avoid a shameful surrender in the village, had no alternative but to beat a hasty retreat.
As the village was surrounded on all sides, at a distance of
about 500 yards, by woods and the Cossacks had already cut off

our obvious line of withdrawal and were advancing on us at a gallop from all directions, we rapidly turned off the main road and tried to reach the woods across country. But before we could get there three-quarters of our force had been lanced from their horses by the Russians, and the remainder suffered a similar fate a few minutes later before they had got well in among the trees. Trying to guard my back against the lance thrusts of my pursuers I repeatedly skirted trees so closely that I was all but brushed from the saddle. At last I succeeded in gaining a little on the nearest Cossacks and already began to hope that I would escape capture when, as I was looking behind me, my horse suddenly stood still and I found myself facing a thicket from which I could see no way out. A quick decision was called for. I leaped from my horse, leaving it to the mercy of the pursuing enemy, slipped into the undergrowth and, speeded by their stabs and shots, continued through it. The brushwood continued to thicken and was soon so dense that no one could possibly have discovered me. So I lay down and kept quiet. Gradually the noise and the shooting died down or receded, from which I concluded that the fate of my companions had largely been sealed. Night fell and I spent it in my thicket in a sombre mood, plagued by hunger, thirst and cold, waiting for the darkness to pass.

At daybreak I left my hiding place and tried to reach a more open part of the forest from where I could attempt a retreat towards Königsbrück. Despite the previous day's confusion I had not, as I discovered later, lost my sense of direction. Gradually the forest became less dense and I continued cautiously on my way for a while. But presently I came upon a broad cart track and as I tried to hurry across, saw a number of Cossacks riding along it who immediately spotted me and set off in pursuit. I

did not have a chance. Any attempt to escape through the wood
at this point where it was so much less dense would have been
futile and would merely have exposed me to even greater danger. So I surrendered without putting up a fight.

Since our departure from the battlefield of Lützen we had
passed through varied country. The plain continues from Lützen through the Altenburg region as far as Rochlitz, dotted
with pretty villages. Around Rochlitz it turns hilly and when
you reach Mittelwayda the hills become mountains. These are
the foothills of the Erz range. From the rich and fertile plain you
enter a poorer and more rugged region whose teeming population is supported less by the fruits of the soil than by the goods its
industries produce. As you approach Tharand the land once
again grows friendlier, a gentler wind blows through the valleys,
the hills are crowned with luxuriant forests. Every step, every
turning reveals a new and usually romantic view. You can almost sense the proximity of the famous Saxon alps. As the traveller emerges from the deep, twisting gorges the little town of
Pirna is revealed in all its charm with the fortress of Sonnen-
stein near by and the lush banks of the Elbe at its feet. From
here as far as Dresden the Elbe valley is full of grace, even if not
as strikingly prosperous as between Dresden and Meissen. Dresden, but lately so peaceful, was now the busy headquarters of
the French, as it had previously been of the Russian and Prussian armies. The French* during their retreat had blasted two
spans of the elegant stone bridge over the river. They had been
temporarily replaced by wooden structures. On the far side of
the Elbe the country is sandy and heavily wooded. The villages

* Presumably a slip of the pen. It was the Prussians and Russians who
blew up the bridge as they retreated, causing a four days' delay to Napoleon
before it could be mended.

are poor and dingy, the small towns less attractive than on the river's western bank.

Like the inhabitants of the Saxon plains those of the Erz mountain range and the Elbe valley had suffered from the constant passage of troops, and everywhere there was a pronounced craving for peace. Though they received us hospitably because we were Germans we had, more often than before, to make do with tokens of goodwill rather than its substance and many of our hosts left us in no doubt that they would have liked us better had we been on the Prussian rather than on the French side.

In general we suffered no hardship though there were days when our rations were in inverse ratio to our exertions. Supplies were procured by bulk requisitioning; individual foraging was strictly forbidden. Our units preserved strict discipline, the French were somewhat laxer and the Italians permitted themselves every kind of excess and were never punished for it.

III

THE Cossacks who had taken me prisoner had been about to mount a picket, so they took me with them to the place chosen for the purpose. There they emptied my pockets, tore off my tunic and asked me where I kept my money. As it happened I had given all I had to my servant the previous day to make some purchases for me in Dresden, so that I was entirely without ready cash. The Cossacks clearly understood my assurances, in sign language, that I had no money on me, but equally clearly did not believe them. They were about to persuade me with blows to reveal my secret treasure when I showed them my watch which they had so far failed to find, and offered it to their leader. This saved me from a beating, and the man to whom I had given the watch also saw to it that I was allowed to keep my boots, which the others had already begun to pull from my legs. Only when they were certain that there was no more loot to be got from me did they begin to interrogate me in sign language, but I avoided answering most of their questions. Then one of the Cossacks produced bread, butter and vodka and I was invited to share their meal. After this breakfast they took me to their squadron commander who had set up his headquarters near Schwegnitz and who, on seeing my uniform which he recognized from the previous day, was delighted with his catch. After some more, rather perfunctory, questioning he sent me on, about an hour's march, to his general who interrogated me in fluent German, asking me my name, rank, the circumstances of my capture, the strength and dispositions of the French army, the location of Napoleon's headquarters, etc., and then sent me straight on to Beresdorf about three hours' journey from Kamenz to the officer commanding the vanguard, General Lanskoy. There, too, I was interrogated closely and then, at nightfall, handed over to a detachment of Cossacks which was returning to the rear with some baggage. But because the route seemed dangerous to them they presently retraced their steps and we spent the night at Beresdorf.

The next morning I was joined by a Saxon sheriff by name of von Carlowitz and his secretary, Conradi, who had also been captured. We were bundled on to a wagon and taken to Baut-zen. Around noon, as we were passing through a village, we met a colonel of Russian lancers who exchanged a few words with us and then took us to the house of the widow of a privy coun-cillor from Berlin, Frau von Glass, where we all had lunch. During the meal, at which we were joined by another Cossack officer of an older vintage, we talked freely and without reserve, and none of the Russians present seemed to think any the worse of me when I confessed that I had taken part in the Russian campaign on the French side. Over coffee the steward of the estate, hearing that my captors had robbed me of my pipe, made me a present of one of his. As a gift it was a trifle, but as a ges-ture it touched me deeply.

In the afternoon we drove on a little while but were soon forced to turn back towards the north-west as far as Wittiche-nau where all three of us spent the night in one room carefully guarded. On the morning of the 16th we were handed over to a squadron of Hussars and, leaving Bautzen on our right, passed through the headquarters of General Blücher. The General in person, in full rig, mounted and smoking a long pipe, watched us go by and made some acid remarks about South Germans still fighting North Germans. This prompted some of the Prussian soldiers who had overheard him to mock and insult us, but their own officers quickly called them to order.

At nightfall we reached Steindörfel, an hour and a half's

journey from Bautzen, where General Count von Wittgenstein *
had his headquarters. Here I was separated from the two Saxon
officials and spent the following day with other prisoners in the
Cossack encampment. That evening, with a transport of some
200 other prisoners, I was taken on foot to Weissenberg and
thence farther to the rear to Würschau, the headquarters of Tsar
Alexander. It was ten o'clock at night by the time we reached
our destination, and for more than an hour we and our escort
awaited further orders. At last they came, to the effect that the
prisoners were to be taken to the bivouac of the Bashkirs and
Kalmuks.† There we were coralled into a tight circle, counted
several times over and then ordered to lie down. The spot was
marshy and quite unsuitable for overnight camping. Nevertheless we were forced to remain prone in the slime and ooze without so much as raising our heads from the moisture; for when-
ever one of us did so a Bashkir would immediately approach and
press him down again saying 'sleep, comrade, sleep'. This was
in some ways the worst night of my life. When dawn broke we
were allowed at least to get up, but several hours elapsed before
we were permitted to light a fire to dry our soaking clothes and
warm our stiff and frozen limbs. At ten o'clock I was brought
before the Tsar's adjutant, General von Wolzogen,‡ who questioned me. He had, in the past, served with the Württemberg
army, a fact of which he made no secret, but did not show the

* The Commander of the Russian forces, successor to the victor of the
Russian campaign, General Kutusov.

† The Bashkirs were a people living south of the Ural mountains. Their
soldiers often wore chain mail and were armed with a bow. The Kalmucks
were a nomadic people living on the northern shore of the Caspian sea.

‡ General Ludwig von Wolzogen was a Prussian who had fought the
campaign of 1805 with Württemberg troops before transferring to the
Russian army.

slightest inclination to make me more comfortable. Returning to the camp I found myself re-united with Herr von Carlowitz and his secretary. It was not long before I was taken to the castle once more, this time to another general who suggested that I should take service with the German legion—a motley body of deserters from the various German contingents of Napoleon's army—pointing out, on the one hand, the advantages I should reap from so doing and on the other, the discomfort and distress to which I would be exposed if I refused. I rejected his offer and was taken back to the encampment. There I was next approached by a French deserter claiming to be a staff officer of field rank by name of Laudon (though I discovered later that he had been a corporal and that his real name was Mercier) who started working on me. But his wheedling and cajoling succeeded no better than the general's more forthright approach.

Towards evening we were passed on to a picket of the Russian militia. These soldiers wore an almost circular cap of felt with the letter 'A' and a cross on it, a brown tunic with a narrow belt, and carried lances as their only weapons. They treated us better than the Bashkirs and Kalmuks had done and did not care in the least whether we spent the night standing, sitting or prone. But the food they provided for us was as unsatisfactory as it had been ever since the beginning of our imprisonment, and I can honestly say that since noon on the 15th I would have warmly welcomed so much as a scrap of horse- or dog-meat.

At last, on the morning of the 19th, we prisoners were taken to the rear. My companions in misfortune were a certain Captain Fischer of General Bertrand's staff and a hundred or so soldiers—Frenchmen, Germans, Italians—some in a pretty desperate state and half naked. Much to our regret we also had to endure the company of Monsieur Laudon. Our escort consisted of a Don-Cossack lieutenant and his sergeant, a Bashkir lieutenant and twenty Bashkirs. The captured officers were provided with transport, the other ranks went on foot. The first day we got as far as the town of Görlitz, on the outskirts of which we camped. Next day we were joined by a number of new prisoners, among them two lieutenants, Colliva and Rompani, of the first Italian infantry regiment of the line. Passing through Lauben, Naumburg and Bunzlau we reached Silesia on 21st May. The following day we rested, and throughout the whole of it heard the sound of heavy gunfire, drawing nearer towards evening, which pleased us as much as it unsettled our escort. Next day we heard that the Russians and Prussians had lost a battle* and were in full retreat towards the river Oder; on the 24th the fleeing baggage train caught up with us and thereafter we were subjected to every kind of insult, not excluding violence, from the rabble comprising the train. We crossed the Oder at Steinau, passed through Winzig, Trachenberg and Suhlau, and on the 26th reached Militsch, the last small town in Silesia, where we again put in a day of rest.

From 20th May onward the officers were billeted at night in houses, and the soldiers locked up in stables and barns. Our lodgings usually consisted of a single room with straw palliasses, a Bashkir spreadeagled inside the room athwart the door and another in the same posture outside. In all our billets we were fed, but only according to our hosts' goodwill. Once installed in our quarters we were not allowed out again, and no one was permitted to leave his vehicle on the march. Once only, at Militsch

---

* Presumably the battle of Bautzen and the subsequent pursuit. It was another victory for Napoleon, but rather a hollow one, as the Russian and Prussian armies were able to retreat in such good order that the French did not have a single trophy to show for their pains.

on the Silesian frontier, were we able to walk about escorted by our Bashkirs. Men in the ranks who fell behind from exhaustion or the need to relieve themselves were driven back into the column with kicks and blows. When their shoes or boots wore out they walked on their bare feet, and after a while there was not a shoe or a boot to be seen among the lot of them. Unable to keep themselves clean they were soon so infested with vermin that the bites nearly drove them mad and of the whole transport only a handful survived the lack of food and clothing and the exertions of the march.

As far as Görlitz and beyond the country was devastated by the war. Görlitz is a lively, bustling town and prettily situated. Lauben and the small Silesian towns beyond are more or less solidly built, the soil is fertile, and flat rather than hilly. In the vicinity of the river Oder and especially on its far side it is sandy. The villages have a tidy and prosperous air. As you approach the Polish frontier the sandiness of the soil becomes more marked and towns and villages look shabbier. Militsch, which belongs to the Counts of Malzahn, has a pretty palace and a beautiful park.

The inhabitants of Lusatia took hardly any interest in us, being far too preoccupied with their own woes. In Lauben a few people showed sympathy with us when we were insulted by Prussian guardsmen. The Silesians I found, as I had expected, boiling over with hatred of the French and their allies. I carefully concealed the fact that I was a Württemberger, feeling much safer as long as I was mistaken for a Frenchman. The fury of the inhabitants often exploded into the most violent abuse, and once I saw a well-dressed and obviously educated man go so far as to vent his spleen physically on some of the poor prisoners. On several occasions, in fact, our escort had to take on the role of protectors.

On 28th May we continued our march, entering the Duchy of Warsaw after a few days' travel. We had another rest day in the neighbourhood of Kalisch. By way of Turek, Hilodawa and Dumbrowicz we reached Plötz on the Vistula on 12th June, and thence continued via Plonsk, Nowe Miasto, Pultusk, Rozan, Lomza, Tykocyn and Knyszyn, the first small Polish–Russian town on our route. We reached Bialystok on 5th July, and Grodno on the Niemen on the 12th.

The number of my companions in misfortune had fluctuated widely between 28th March and 12th July. Several non-commissioned officers and men had died on the way, others had fallen sick and been left in hospitals. At several halts convalescents had been added to our transport. Of the officers, Captain Fischer had escaped at Czatowpansky on the evening of 3rd June with our knowledge and assistance and at Tykocyn, on 2nd July Lieutenants Colliva and Rompani had followed his example. I never heard what happened to the two Italians, but Captain Fischer I met ten years later in Stuttgart where he happened to be spending a few days. After the escape of these three I was left alone with the repulsive so-called Adjutant or Major Laudon. Weeping and laughing in turn, begging and threatening, he continued to try to tempt me into the German legion. Repeatedly he showed signs of insanity, sometimes culminating in physical violence, changing abruptly to self-pity when I forcibly restrained him. The escape of Fischer had already put our Cossack lieutenant in a vile temper, and that of Colliva and Rompani infuriated him even more. Yet on each occasion it was not long before he was pacified. In Bialystok, however, to our great regret, he was relieved of his command because of these two incidents—an event he had predicted. This very fair and decent Cossack was called Elia Vassilievich—I have forgotten his

I

surname. His successor was a lieutenant of the Fourth Infantry Regiment.

Another transport of prisoners was travelling along the same road as we, comprising a large proportion of officers, mostly French and Italian. On several occasions we spent the night in the same village, and never failed to visit each other, partly to find a new audience for our tales of woe and partly to enliven and diversify our conversation. We tried repeatedly to persuade our respective transport commandants to join forces, but this would have meant that one or the other had to surrender his command—something which neither was prepared to do. Among the officers of the other transport I renewed my acquaintance with Count Mirelli, the commander of our ill-fated patrol to Schwegnitz. He told me that he had also been taken prisoner the day of our disastrous reconnaissance after receiving several wounds from lance thrusts. Another prisoner was Baron de Montaran, equerry to the French Emperor, who had been captured near Gotha. Montaran, a very polished Parisian, found his lot particularly hard to bear, but he was a man of excellent mettle who maintained his morale throughout. I came across him a number of times later and in Czernigov he did me signal service. A third officer I met was Lieutenant Pechin of the 23rd Regiment, a young man who endeared himself to us all by his unquenchable optimism and good humour. In Bialystok we ran into a number of Saxon officers who had been captured during the retreat from Moscow and had recently been returned this far westward from the interior so as to be released and repatriated as soon as Saxony changed sides and joined the Russian cause. They were only too eager to tell us the tale of their captivity and so give us an inkling of what was in store for us. Yet though their stories were hardly reassuring they did not greatly add to our apprehensions, leading us rather to believe that our lot was likely to improve the farther we got away from the scene of the 1812 campaign. One of these Saxon prisoners, staff surgeon Hellermann, gave me a letter of introduction to the Minsk district medical officer, Doctor Schmidt, which later stood me in excellent stead and put me greatly in the debt of both these good people.

During this sixteen-week period of our travels as prisoners of war we had had a few good days as well as many bad ones. All along our journey through the Duchy of Warsaw we passed Russian units on their way to the front, and they never left us in any doubt about their anger and resentment at the sight of us. Having run this gauntlet comparatively unscathed, we were then exposed to the hatred and insults of the Russian garrisons stationed in nearly every Polish town and village where we spent the night. At our very first staging post there was an incident which boded ill for the future. We met a Russian colonel by name of Krukenikov. At first he treated us quite politely, but later he approached the barn where the men were quartered and in very good French called for a few Frenchmen to come forward. Two volunteers appeared at the door and courteously put themselves at his disposal, whereupon he hurled himself at them with a stream of curses and sword drawn, and could infallibly have murdered them had not the Bashkir guard and our Cossack lieutenant, who fortunately happened to be at hand, intervened and restrained him. Even the Russian soldiers who had come running at the hubbub showed their indignation at what had happened, and they and the Cossack officer roundly and volubly condemned the colonel's behaviour. They did their best to reassure us, but as far as this barbaric officer was concerned the incident did not end there. Having been dismissed from the army as insane, and returning home by the same route that we were travelling, he pursued our transport for several days, wounding, in Ostrow, the so-called Major Laudon with sword and fists and pursuing several others through the streets at the point of his sword. It was only in Kalisch that our and the Cossack officer's complaints succeeded in having him arrested for a few days, after which we saw no more of him. This was by no means the only evidence we had of the Russians' hatred of us, but never again did it manifest itself in quite so violent a fashion.

The behaviour of the Poles towards us was very different from that of the Silesians. Wherever we went they showed us the greatest courtesy and kindness, deploring the present political situation and candidly expressing their hopes of a rapid restoration of French rule. The Russians strongly disapproved of these sentiments and in particular of their open expression, but they could hardly isolate us from all contact with the local population, who in any case were usually sensible enough to moderate their language in the hearing of their enemies. In the villages we passed through we were usually quartered in the manor house, where the squire served us with the best his kitchen and cellar could provide. Our men were also secretly supplied with whatever delicacies were available and could most easily be concealed. In the towns we were not so well provided but there, too, we usually found some, be it noblemen, officials or ordinary citizens, who would do what they could to improve our lot—often simply by buying us a decent meal and a few drinks at an inn. Nor was this all the good Poles did for us. Though they offered us no money, knowing very well that we would refuse it, they often provided us with clothes and linen of which we were greatly in need. At the very first Polish village where we had a day of rest, Faliszewo, the daughter of a certain Herr von Grumkewicz, made me a shirt. In Plonsk a young lady of excellent family even offered to help Lieutenant Pechin to escape and to take his place as a prisoner of war. The Lieutenant, deeply touched, naturally declined the offer. Quite often on our march through a village we would be stopped by the squire, and on one occasion even by the squire's lady, with offers of refreshment which enabled us to last the rest of the day without further nourishment. Jewish hosts accorded us a cooler welcome. Not only did they make us pay for everything that we consumed—lodgings excepted—but even so showed us in no uncertain manner how reluctant they were to have to put up with us at all. Many expressed great fear of the possible return of the French, for which they probably had excellent cause. But there were also some who were differently disposed, had no such fears and, out of a sense of common humanity, treated us kindly. The universal Polish problem of dirt bothered us less than formerly—partly because by now we had become accustomed to it and it offended us less, and partly because we were usually fortunate enough to be billeted in the best houses. On the banks of the Vistula, however, I once more came, as I had done the previous year, across the disgusting disease called the Vistula pig-tail. The hairs of the head become glued together and in this condition must on no account be cut off as this, it is said, inevitably produces consumption. Those afflicted with the disease are debilitated and of a pale, greasy complexion. Usually the diseased hair falls out in the course of years and the patient then recovers, but in some cases the victim is relieved of his burden only by death. The sickness is rarer among Poles than it is among Jews, and its cause may well be found—apart from local circumstances—in the appalling filth in which these people live.

We usually conversed with the local gentry either in French

or in German. If, as rarely happened, the squire knew neither of these two languages, a smattering of Latin was likely to be of use. If nothing else availed there were always the Jews, all of whom speak, apart from the local language, a very corrupt kind of German which they regard as their mother tongue.*

From the day we set foot in the Duchy of Warsaw, every officer received for his subsistence half a Prussian thaler (50 groschen) † per day payable every five days. In a country where we were housed and fed free wherever we went this pittance was not only sufficient to provide for our daily needs but even allowed us to put by a small capital for a rainy day. This precaution soon had its reward, for as soon as we reached Russian Poland we were told flatly that henceforth we would be paid according to the Russian rate, which meant that we received every day half a rouble in paper money (i.e. 14 groschen). The blow was severe, but the Saxon officers in Bialystok assured us that we would find the sum perfectly adequate in the Russian interior and that on our journey there we would undoubtedly often find quarters where we could get our food, if not free, at least very cheaply indeed.

* i.e. Yiddish. The French had no better opinion of East European Jews than Vossler. Ségur, after a detailed and extremely disparaging description of those he encountered in Lithuania, concludes: 'Everything except their filthiness distinguishes them from the Lithuanian peasants. Their every aspect indicates a dishonoured people.' But, like Vossler, he found that they had their uses. In Russia, where none were to be found, he grumbles: 'Though the eye is no longer offended by their disgusting presence it must regretfully be admitted that they were missed in other respects. In particular we missed their lively and industrious selfishness from which almost anything could be obtained in return for cash, and their broken German—the only language we were able to understand in that wilderness.'

† Very roughly five shillings in present-day purchasing power.

The countryside from the Silesian border as far as the Niemen is generally flat, never more than mildly hilly, and usually of sandy or at any rate light soil. In parts, for instance around Pultusk, it is densely wooded. Husbandry is almost the sole means of subsistence for the inhabitants, cattle breeding of no great consequence, nor horse-breeding either. Factories or even cottage industries are non-existent and trade is restricted to the scarce local produce. The artisans are mostly Jewish, as are most of the inn-keepers. The villages are squalid and their inhabitants miserably poor—as I have mentioned before. The towns, on the other hand, present a somewhat more prosperous appearance and some, such as Kalisch, Plonsk and Lomza, can even bear comparison with the better East-Prussian towns. Bialystok is rather a pleasant little place but it, too, like the others I have mentioned, owes its comparatively impressive appearance to the period of Prussian rule.

IV

BY the time we reached Grodno my health had broken down. For the last fortnight I had been suffering from an inflammation of the eyes, caused partly by the heat but mainly by drifting sand, which threatened to rob me of my sight. A doctor whom I consulted about it advised me to petition the town's civilian Governor, Privy Councillor Leschern, for permission to stay in Grodno till I was cured. He took the trouble to escort me in person to the Governor and to support my application which was consequently granted. Leaving the Governor's residence I ran into a Russian official who questioned me about my situation, speaking German with a northern accent. Straightaway he took me to his home for luncheon, and ignoring the displeasure of his compatriots, invited me to make free of his table for the remainder of my stay. I accepted his offer most gratefully. This generous individual's name was Bagemühl, he was a Prussian by birth and was employed by the local government as an architect. My billet I had made with a German cabinet-maker, where I occupied a clean, pleasant room. The well-ordered life of Grodno had a favourable effect not only on my eye trouble, which was being treated by the Saxon Chief Surgeon Richter, but also on my general condition. Socially, too, my stay provided me with a number of amenities. I spent many happy hours at the Bagemühls, though his matrimonial quarrels caused me occasional embarrassment. Bagemühl also introduced me to an elderly major, by name of von Roth, a native of Zweibrücken, who encouraged me to visit him often and treated me with the utmost consideration. I was, moreover, on the best of terms with a number of other officer prisoners of war, among them Lieutenant Pechin whom I have mentioned before and who had also been granted permission to stay in Grodno for a while, and a Lieutenant Böcker, of Napoleon's guard of Lancers. Another acquaintance who had joined our company in Bialystok was the Württemberg Court Courier Lang, and several Saxon doctors completed our circle. On 26th July we were joined by two Württembergers: the Secretary in the War Ministry Krais and Lieutenant von Bragnato, both of whom had been taken prisoner in Silesia.

Grodno is the seat of a civilian governor. The town is sizeable and has a number of well-constructed houses and streets. The Christian inhabitants are mainly Poles, there are a few Russians but somewhat more Germans. The latter treated us with cold reserve, and as for the Russians, we ourselves avoided their company as far as possible. The Poles, however, showed us a good deal of sympathy. The Jews, here as everywhere, lived only for their one god: Mammon. Grodno is prettily though not spectacularly situated. The river on which it lies is navigable and brings commerce and employment to the people.

About the middle of the month of August, when my eyes were still not fully cured, I committed the indiscretion of asking Councillor Riesenkopf, who was responsible for paying the prisoners of war their wages, for better quarters. Not only did he refuse my request but also gave me the cheerless assurance that he would make it his business to have me packed off, without fail, by the very next transport to leave Grodno for the interior. My personal appeals to the Governor were as fruitless as the efforts on my behalf of a lady of quality, and I was accordingly attached to a consignment of prisoners which left for Minsk on 19th August.

With a heavy heart I took leave of the Bagemühls, of Major von Roth and of my other acquaintances in Grodno and left the town accompanied only by their best wishes for my future.

A number of my companions, including Count Mirelli, Lieutenants Böckler, Pechin, Hartemenk and Kernerlink, as well as Court Courier Lang had already left with an earlier transport. My travelling companions were Krais and Bragnato, as well as the ineffable Laudon and a French servant who claimed to be an aide-de-camp of Prince Poniatowsky* and called himself Normann—a nasty, ill-tempered and thoroughly unreliable character. There were some 200 or 250 other ranks and our escort consisted of one infantry lieutenant and 18 men of the Fourth Infantry Regiment and 30 peasant Cossacks from Poltawa.

Our route led through Skidel, Kamienka, Zeludok, Belica, Novogrudok, Mir and Koydonovo, and on 7th September we reached a village on the outskirts of Minsk, having marched a total of eighty-four hours. The commander of our transport had greatly aggravated our sufferings en route—not so much by malice or ill-will as by gross carelessness and neglect of duty. He was constantly drunk and thereby completely forfeited the respect of his subordinates. His orders were executed either indifferently or not at all, and the unfortunate prisoners were exposed, during the periods when he was incapable, to a greater or lesser degree of ill-treatment at the hands of his men, of the local population and of those on whom they were billeted. Throughout the march we stayed mainly at Jewish inns, once or twice with peasants but never with gentry. Our lodgings were

* Polish prince and patriot with a most distinguished military record in defence of his country's freedom. He joined the French when Napoleon promised to liberate Poland and became war minister of the Duchy of Warsaw. He played a prominent part as Corps commander in the Russian campaign of 1812 and was made a Marshal of France after the battle of Leipzig in 1813.

always free of charge, our food and drink, however, we had to pay for, sometimes at exorbitant prices. There were occasions when the local inhabitants would not have provided us with victuals even against payment had not the transport commandant asserted his authority. In these circumstances it was not surprising that we arrived in Minsk with empty pockets and half starved. The people of the places through which we passed were all quite indifferent to our sufferings—they even treated us harshly, and we found only one person who showed us, not only common humanity but real warmth of feeling. This was the mayor of Novogrudok, who saw to it that we were fed free of charge. I must also mention a member of the Russian army whom we met in Swierno, a certain Colonel de Fries, who enquired solicitously about our well-being and made our stay there comparatively pleasant by prevailing upon the local squire, a friend of his, to invite us to dinner.

The countryside between Grodno and Minsk is in character with most of the rest of Poland. The villages are generally squalid and their inhabitants resemble them. The small towns are somewhat more attractive but not so much so as those that once lived under Prussian rule. There are some fine manor houses and country seats, chief among them the estates of Count von Tiesenhausen in and around Zeludok.

My eye trouble gradually mended during the march, but it had left a weakness which prevented me from reading for more than half an hour at a stretch. For the rest, my state of health, apart from the diarrhoea which had plagued me for so long but had lost much of its virulence, was fairly good. But on 3rd September I fell ill with what soon turned out to be a genuine attack of typhoid fever accompanied by violent diarrhoea. As the transport did not boast a doctor (who in any case would have been of little use in view of the absence of medicines) the illness had to take its course until we reached Minsk. There Lieutenant von Bragnato tried to have me admitted to hospital, but he succeeded only after I had returned from the very brink of the grave, thanks to the strength of my constitution and the help of some medicaments which Doctor Schmidt of Minsk had provided for me. At last, on 12th September, I was taken to hospital where I was lodged in a room with several French officers, some of them sick, some wounded, and all very full of their own woes.

Thanks to excellent treatment by the hospital doctor, to whom Doctor Schmidt had specially commended me, I was soon so far restored that I was able to leave my room and accept Doctor Schmidt's invitation to take my meals in his house. There I was fed a suitable and nourishing diet, sparingly at first but gradually increasing in quantity, and after a fortnight I had completely recovered.

Doctor Schmidt, a native of Geislingen in Württemberg, and his wife, *née* Willmann from Willingen in the Duchy of Baden, were justly famous throughout Russia for the generosity and sympathy with which they tried to lighten the burdens of prisoners of war, notably their German compatriots' and most particularly, of course, in the case of fellow-Württembergers. No amount of Russian disapproval could deflect them from this mission. I and many, many other Württemberg and Baden soldiers, Germans in general and Frenchmen too, gratefully recall the kindness of this truly noble couple.

The city of Minsk is the seat of a provincial government, densely populated and generally well built. The cathedral is an architectural masterpiece. The town is pleasantly situated and inhabited mainly by Poles, with only a sprinkling of true

Russians. There are large numbers of Jews, and it was here that I found them most bitter against the French and their allies.

During our stay in Minsk we were, to my great delight, relieved of the company of Messrs Laudon and Normann, who had joined the German legion. In their place our numbers were substantially increased by the arrival of Major Löffler, Captains von Brunow and von Butsch, and Lieutenants Hölder and Röll, all of them Württembergers who had been captured at the battle of Bautzen. Other new arrivals included the Bavarian Lieutenant von Michel, of the second light infantry battalion, and Surgeon Stör. All the various transports of prisoners of war that arrived in Minsk during this time were merged into one and then despatched to Czernigov, our next major staging post.

V

OUR departure had been fixed for 27th September. Before setting off we bade a warm and grateful farewell to the Schmidt family who, out of the goodness of their hearts, made me a present of a new shirt and a loan of twenty-five roubles.

Apart from the Württemberg and Bavarian officers already mentioned, my travelling companions were Commissioner Krais and Lieutenant von Bagki, an intelligent but devious individual known to be strongly anti-Russian and therefore being deported into the interior, the Polish Lieutenant von Ninewski, and a number of Frenchmen, including Equerry Baron de Montaran, Captains Vannacker, Fanchon, Carlier, Glaise, and Lieutenants Leon, George, Dubois, Blanc, etc. Altogether we were 37 officers and some 300 other ranks. Our escort consisted of a good-natured Cossack lieutenant, two Bashkir lieutenants, two infantry officers, two Cossacks, 50 Bashkirs and some 80 militiamen—nick-named peasant crusaders.

In this company we set out, on 27th September, towards the provincial capital of Czernigov, about 150 hours' march away in the direction of Kiev, resting every third or fourth day. On 6th October we reached the fortress of Bobruisk, situated on the Berezina of vivid and unhappy memory. There we saw, without much joy, two Württemberg cannons the Russians had captured in an engagement near Koydonovo, ten miles from Minsk. We also met a Württemberg assistant surgeon by name of Dertinger who had been set to work in the local hospital. On 12th October we reached Rogaczev on the Dnieper, crossed the river Sor on the 19th and on the 20th spent our last night in Russian Poland. The following night found us bivouacking in the village of Dobrianka, in Russia proper, and on the 28th we reached Czernigov, though we were not allowed to make our quarters there but in a small hamlet about two miles beyond.

Throughout this march from Minsk to Czernigov we endured much hardship. Often our horses were too weak to carry us and we had to continue on foot. The weather was changeable, at times very blustery and cold. Heavy rains had made the roads impassable. At night we were furnished only with a roof over our heads, and our so-called salaries were often barely enough to buy us a crust of dry bread and a handful of onions. Our clothes were shabby, our linen in shreds, though we mended both as best we could and washed the linen on the days we rested. Everywhere the inhabitants treated us with undisguised hostility, often culminating in murderous attacks on anyone who strayed from the column. In Rogaczev we would all have been put to death by the Jewish inhabitants had we not had our escort. In Dobrianka a similar fate threatened us, and only the resolute action of the transport commandant, who threatened to open fire on the peasant mob, saved us. So it was with considerable relief that we saw the church spires of Czernigov, where we hoped to find a quieter and more peaceful atmosphere.

The countryside around Minsk is generally dismal, much of it covered with swamps and dank forests. The villages are drab, the inhabitants shabby. The towns are mostly dilapidated and only a few contain a decent building or two—usually the church or monastery and very rarely private houses. Manors are less frequent, and unlike in Poland every village does not have its own squire. The houses as far as the border with Russia proper are usually squalid, with one large room inhabited by man and beast. In the former Polish towns and villages live large numbers of Jews, who are cleaner here than on the Vistula. The large and populous village of Dobrianka, the first on the Russian side of the border, provides a striking contrast with the places on the Polish side. Here the houses, though also of log construction, are more roomy, comfortable and neat. The windows have glass panes in them, a decent stove warms the communal living room, tables and benches are more solidly built and scrubbed clean, the floor, no longer covered in dried dung, is neatly swept and strewn with sand. The alcoves are separated from the living quarters. In a corner by the door hangs an ikon, before which the inhabitants bow every time they enter or leave the house. The livestock is stabled apart and not so much as a chicken is allowed inside the house. The entrance to the living room leads through a lobby which contains the kitchen. The master of the house wears a long beard, his dress consists of a coat reaching down to his knees, buttonless and gathered at the waist by a belt. The trousers are baggy, the feet encased in high boots. The women wear a white or coloured kerchief over their heads, and an attractive blouse whose appearance is spoilt only by being belted across the bosom. Their skirts are woollen, white, grey or blue, the shoes of Muscovy hide. The children wear woollen coats or jackets and all have boots or shoes. The clothes are kept clean and neat. Of their diet I know nothing, for these people never ate in our presence. Most of them regarded us with horror, and wherever we were billeted the ikons were quickly removed from the living rooms as soon as we entered, and hidden away. Though the other villages through which we passed on our way to Czernigov cannot compare in prosperity with Dobrianka, we noted everywhere, much to our satisfaction, that the Russians pay a great deal more attention to cleanliness than do their Polish neighbours.

In the hamlet outside Czernigov where we were accommo-

dated our quarters were shabby to a degree, and our nourishment barely above starvation level. We spent most of the daylight hours in the town, but by nightfall had to be back in our village. We suffered great boredom during the long evenings, the more so since the inhabitants' open hostility made it inadvisable for us to leave our billets after dark. The villagers, on the other hand, often assembled in one or other of the houses where we were staying, where they discussed with great animation matters of which we were totally ignorant. Once, however, we witnessed a family feast, at which vodka flowed freely and which ended with all the participants roaring drunk. On another occasion the young people of the village took it into their heads to put on the weirdest masks imaginable and to parade in them from house to house.* In my own billet I once attended the conclusion of a marriage contract during which the young couple kept very quiet and passive while their elders spoke animatedly on their behalf and finally shook hands vigorously all round. One morning at daybreak—it was the 10th of November —several drunken peasants armed with cudgels appeared at the billet I shared with Captain von Butsch. They roused us from our palliasses and with unmistakable gestures gave us to understand that they wanted to be rid of us and that we had better move on quickly if we valued life and limb. In every other billet in the village similar scenes were being enacted at the very same moment. So we hurriedly set off together for Czernigov, where we complained to the Governor, the Commandant, the Mayor and the Chief of Police, but all in vain. Weary of being sent from

* Remembering that Vossler and his companions stayed in this village from 28th October until 11th November, this sounds very much like celebrations of Halloween (31st October). Vossler, coming from a Protestant country, would be unfamiliar with the custom.

K

pillar to post we returned to our hamlet in the evening and intimated to our unwilling hosts that we would be leaving them for good the next morning. With that they left us in peace overnight and allowed us to depart in good order the following day.

VI

I N Czernigov we rented quarters privately and at our own expense since nobody was prepared to provide any for us. With Captain von Butsch and Commissioner Krais I found a room with a stove at a cobbler's which, together with the necessary firewood for heating and cooking, cost us half of our combined daily income. Here we installed ourselves as comfortably as we could—that is to say we bought hay on which to sleep, a glass tumbler each, an iron cauldron and a copper coffee pot for us all as well as a tin spoon, a knife and a wooden dish each. To serve us we adopted two Württemberg soldiers who would otherwise have perished of starvation and who, by this arrangement, at least were sure of a meal.

We spent ten weeks in Czernigov, from 11th November 1813 to 19th January 1814. Our circle of acquaintances was enlarged by a number of fellow countrymen, including Regimental Surgeon Pommer, War Commissioner Keller, Courier Lang and Assistant Surgeon Bopp. Five miles outside the town another Württemberger, Assistant Surgeon Mautz, lived at the manor of a wealthy and active widow in the capacity of medical and general adviser. These people had all been established for some time where we found them. The regimental surgeon and the war commissioner lived in the main hospital as guests of a German apothecary and had every reason to be satisfied with their situation. Assistant Surgeon Bopp had established a medical practice which provided him with an income far in excess of ours. All these early arrivals vied with each other in their efforts to be of service to us. They acquainted us with local conditions and reconciled us as far as possible to our fate. We Württembergers met regularly every day, sometimes at each other's lodgings, otherwise at an inn of which I shall have occasion to write more later. The talk was mainly of our chances of an early return home on which all our hopes were fixed. Another subject, for the time being of equal importance, was the problem of keeping alive, and if the thought of home always raised our spirits that of our present condition tended to depress them. Our group was augmented and frequently enlivened by a number of Bavarians. With the French we had little contact, and they for their part studiously avoided us as soon as the defection of Württemberg from the French cause became known. I did, however, often visit Baron de Montaran, the imperial equerry, who was kept in funds from St Petersburg and so was able to lead a comfortable existence. From his comparative affluence he occasionally treated me and Lieutenant Pechin, who stayed in Czernigov rather longer than the rest of us, to a good meal. At home, where we spent most of our mornings, we occupied ourselves with a variety of chores. The first task on rising was a careful search of our linen for the vermin we had acquired on our travels and of which, with the best will in the world, we were never able to rid ourselves entirely. After breakfast, consisting of coffee and good white bread, we mended our clothes, darned our underwear, and usually spent the rest of the morning reading German books which Mautz made available to us from his wealthy widow's library. At noon we lunched. A scrap of beef cooked with potatoes and yellow turnips in the iron cauldron was our modest menu, day-in day-out, as long as our stay in Czernigov lasted. Yet we never suffered from lack of appetite, nor even sickened of the monotonous fare, for there was never enough of it on the table. Our drink consisted of a jug of Kvass, concocted from crushed barley, water and yeast. In the afternoon we paid and received visits, went for walks in the town and its surroundings, and at nightfall assembled at a certain inn where we dined on a piece of bread, occasionally an egg or two, and a glass of warm tea with brandy. At eight o'clock we returned to our quarters and retired to bed.

My health during my stay in Czernigov was quite passable, and if occasionally I suffered from stomach pains they never became intolerable. More disagreeable was my chronic dysentery which compelled me, throughout the winter, to obey the call of nature in the middle of the night under open skies.

The city of Czernigov is a provincial capital and the see of an archbishop. It is situated in a plain a quarter of an hour's journey from the river Desna. The surroundings are monotonous and offer little worth seeing. The town straggles over a considerable distance. At its centre rises the citadel, square in shape with turrets at each of its four corners, surrounded by high, blank walls without so much as a loophole in them. It is used only as a prison. On the outskirts of the city lies a large monastery, notable mainly for its trellised tower, where the archbishop lives.

The government offices and the hospital are of stone, all other buildings, even the governor's residence, of wood. Near the citadel there is a big market place along whose centre run two long, colonnaded buildings in which tradesmen, artisans and merchants have their booths, and where they daily display their wares—everything from luxuries to trash—with much lively sales chatter. Among the things you can buy are entire wooden houses for farm labourers. Outside the larger of the two buildings the Jews have set up their stalls where they exchange money of every denomination, paper and coin, and turn a handsome profit. Jews and Christians alike use abaci for doing their sums, manipulating them deftly and accurately for even the most complicated calculations. I was told that only the better educated merchants were able to do sums on paper. Invariably the hucksters in the market overcharge grossly for their goods, but the natives are accustomed to haggling and the stranger soon learns to do likewise. Substantial sums are paid in paper money, with copper coins as small change the largest of which, a Pietak, is as big as a Brabant dollar and worth about 1½ farthings. Silver coins are not common and gold ones very rare. The town's wooden houses generally stand some way back from the street and are surrounded by courtyards enclosed with wooden fences. They are all single-storied, so that they remain largely invisible behind their high fencing. As in Poland, the houses are without privies, the yard as a whole serving this purpose. This does not make it more filthy than it would otherwise be because of the pigs that run about in it and eat the excrement. Indeed, so greedy are they for this fare that in order to obey the call of nature in peace you need a stout stick to ward them off.

Near the market place are several inns where spirits, tea and barley beer are served as well as various kinds of meat, ready cooked and heaped high on counters, which is warmed up when ordered. There is usually also a variety of fish available which is sold in large quantities in the market and eaten by the Russians on their frequent fast days fried in flour and oil. In the matter of cleanliness the inns can bear no comparison with their German counterparts, and in all of them patrons must expect to be infested with vermin. Visitors who stay the night are provided with a straw palliasse along the wall of a common room. One of these inns we frequented regularly, and because of the filthy appearance of its host and his two bearded waiters, all of whom, incidentally, were most attentive to our wishes, we christened it 'The Three Mudlarks'. A wine shop—the only one in town— we visited once only. It was cleaner than the inns and more comfortably furnished. The wine served in this establishment came from the region of the Moldau river, but it cost more than we could afford.

There are several churches in Czernigov, but only three of them of stone. The others are built entirely of wood. On Christmas day we attended divine service in the cathedral. The rites of the Russian Orthodox Church are very splendid, the singing of the choir was magnificent and we were entranced by the glorious rendering of the anthem.

The town's streets are neither cobbled nor paved, and as a result very uneven and in wet weather so muddy that I saw even carriages with powerful teams get stuck. The inhabitants throw all their refuse in the street, and even in the main thoroughfares one comes across dead cats, dogs, and even horses and cattle. Especially repulsive and annoying is the large number of stray dogs. They roam the streets in packs and not only bark at passers-by but sometimes actually attack them. This happened to us repeatedly, and we had difficulty in defending ourselves, though if there are only a few of them a sharp blow or two from a stick landing on the foremost and boldest is usually enough to make the rest beat a howling retreat. At night we never ventured out singly but only in groups, for fear of being set upon and murdered, which happened to several Frenchmen while we were there. Though Czernigov boasts a police force which goes the rounds of the city at night its responsibility did not appear to extend to us poor prisoners of war. On the contrary, we suspected the police of aiding and abetting the murderers of the Frenchmen. They certainly fined every prisoner of war they caught in the streets after dark.

All the time we were there Czernigov had a garrison of no more than two companies, and those mostly invalids. The men were billeted on the citizenry and the officers rented their own lodgings. The officers were anything but well bred. Discipline seemed rather lax. The inhabitants of Czernigov are not Russians proper, but a mixture of Russians and Poles and have, as so often happens on the borders between two great nations, largely abandoned their respective national virtues and adopted by way of compensation their vices instead. They are sly and cunning, greedy and deceitful. The weaker sex, which among the lower classes can rarely be described as beautiful either in Russia or in Poland, is here downright ugly, dirty, and excessively contentious and quarrelsome. Both sexes showed themselves hard and pitiless towards the unfortunate prisoners of war, the women even more so than the men. There are many artisans in the town but most of them not very skilled. Others make a living out of trade and commerce. Were they better educated their industry and perseverance might quickly raise them to a higher standard of life. Officials and gentry are rare and, as far as we in our position were able to judge, not particularly cultured. Neither group ever condescended to any social contacts with us. The Jews, of whom there are a great number, live by trade and commerce and are distinguished here as in Poland by their industry and greed. The naturalized foreigners are mostly Germans; artisans and professional people, apothecaries and doctors, all of them making a comfortable living, which they fully earn by their diligence, thrift and honesty. Their often cold and distant behaviour towards us was sufficiently explained by the suspicion with which the Russians viewed their contacts with prisoners of war.

The dress of the upper classes is entirely French in cut and fashion while that of the lower classes is indistinguishable from the peasants'. The people's way of life is simple. There are no public entertainments of any kind such as dances. In some of the gentry's houses there were occasional balls and suppers. The food of the middle classes consists of meat and farinaceous dishes, on days of fasting of salt fish and eggs fried in oil. The common people subsist on gruel, sauerkraut and salt fish, and during Lent almost entirely on fish. Food is cheap, and bread is only one third of its price in Germany. The same goes for beef and mutton, green and root vegetables, potatoes and onions. The market is always well stocked with every kind of food. The universal drink is barley beer and tea. At all hours of the day bearded Russians wander the streets of the town crying their wares of beer and tea. The latter they carry on their backs in large containers to whose base a sort of charcoal burner is attached which keeps the drink piping hot. For sweetening they use honey in place of sugar.

The winter we spent in Czernigov was not severe, starting only half-way through November, and though we never had less than three or four degrees of frost the temperature rarely fell below ten or twelve degrees. The news of Württemberg's defection from France and alliance with Russia, Prussia and Austria reached Czernigov as early as 14th November. We heard it from a resident doctor with whom we were on friendly terms. In the first flush of relief we hurried to the governor and claimed treatment appropriate to our new status as allies. But he prevaricated, pleading lack of instructions from the central government, and the only concession we succeeded in wringing from him was a promise that for the time being we would not be packed off to Kursk with the next transport of prisoners. Even this partial success raised our spirits and filled us with confidence. From then on not a day passed without our calling on the governor and eagerly enquiring about the receipt of orders for our return home. But we were kept on the rack of uncertainty for another fortnight. At last, at the end of November, he summoned us to let us know that the relevant instructions had now arrived, but that our departure from Czernigov would be delayed for some time yet as he would have to assemble all the Bavarians and Württembergers in the province. He would not even consider an increase in our miserable wages, far less an advance of pay. There is no need to stress our aggravation at this delay, but we took comfort from the knowledge that we had advanced a long way on the road to our ultimate goal. Yet though we made every effort to expedite our journey we found the Russian authorities far less interested in the matter than we were and had to put up with endless procrastination.

A pleasant surprise during this period of impatient waiting was the payment of 100 paper roubles to every officer for the purchase of winter clothing, which relieved us of much worry and anxiety. At the beginning of January 1814 a second order for our speedy repatriation arrived, and at last serious efforts were made to expedite our departure. On 13th January a militia officer was appointed to accompany us and the date of our departure fixed for the 19th. We would gladly have done without the escort, the more so since we had learned from reliable sources that the officer concerned had instructions not to trust us and to keep us under strict surveillance. But our efforts in this direction remained fruitless and so we resigned ourselves to still being marshalled and transported like prisoners, however valid our claim to better treatment. The Russian authorities, in fact, either would not or could not understand why we were so eager to leave, since to their way of thinking our condition in Czernigov was very comfortable. The day before our departure—the 18th January—we were privileged to witness the rare spectacle of the blessing of the water. Surrounded by his clergy and excellent choir, accompanied by all the civil and military dignitaries of the town and in the presence of a vast multitude of all classes the archbishop in full vestments blessed the small brook that flows past the city. The ice that still covered it had been hacked open for the ceremony, which was accompanied by the thunder of cannon and performed with many prayers and great solemnity. When it was over, those of the Greek Orthodox faith scooped up some of the consecrated water, the rest of the day being spent in prayer and meditation.

VII

ON 19th January we saw the sun rise on Czernigov for the last time. At daybreak we joyfully assembled in a square where, after some delay, the sleighs in which the officers were to travel also arrived. Doctors Bopp and Mautz were classed as officers for this purpose. The latter had taken a reluctant leave of his lady, rejecting several highly advantageous inducements to prolong his stay. He and Bopp were well supplied with money and provisions. We were joined by a number of Bavarians, Westphalians and Hessians.* The non-commissioned officers and men were mostly Württembergers. The entire transport, including officers, numbered about 130. At ten o'clock in the morning we set out in high spirits. The officers were under orders to keep pace with and observe the same halts as the men—an arrangement which was bound greatly to delay our journey and against which we fully intended to protest as soon as we could find a military commandant who would give the officers permission to speed up their pace. We took the road to Bobruisk and made short marches. No more than three days out of Czernigov, on 21st January, we were forced, to our great annoyance, to put in a day of rest. Our objections fell on deaf ears. By way of Lokiev, Reczice, Gorval and Pobolova we travelled mostly through forests, often accompanied by packs of howling wolves, and reached Bobruisk on 2nd February, having put in another three days' rest on the way. All along the route we had been treated with some degree of courtesy once the inhabitants discovered that we had turned from enemies into allies. Only the con-

---

* By the autumn of 1813, with Napoleon's fortunes clearly on the wane, most of his German allies had deserted him and gone over to the other side. The Saxons stayed faithful longest, switching sides only during the great battle of Leipzig.

founded militia officer and his crew refused to make any concessions to this fact.

In Bobruisk we spent another rest day and used it to complain to the local commandant, Colonel Bergmann, about the method of our transportation and the behaviour of the militia officer. Our complaints were recognized as justified and we were immediately removed from the command of this officer. The men it is true, remained under his orders, but he was given strict instructions to treat them better. As for the officers, one of us— Lieutenant-Colonel von Berndes—was appointed our leader and we were given as our escort two tough, willing and well-behaved Cossacks. Passports and other papers were entrusted to Lieutenant-Colonel von Berndes and only the route of march to one of the Cossacks. So, on 4th February, we parted company with our men who continued on foot, and resumed our journey by sleigh. Captain von Butsch and I had bought one, on our first day of rest at Riepki, which gave us good protection against the cold.

On the very first day we almost regretted parting with our militia officer, for we found ourselves abominably served with horses. But the next day our Cossacks remedied this defect and from then on we ourselves saw to it, where necessary by the use of threats, that the local authorities provided us with sound animals for the next stage of our journey.

We made rapid progress and after a few days our Cossacks found themselves compelled to abandon their horses and to make use, as we did, of sleighs. On 5th February, at Glusk, we fell in with some Bavarian and Saxon officers who had been held prisoners of war in the province of Nishny-Novgorod and had started their return journey as long ago as 29th November. They could not praise too highly the energy and despatch with which the provincial governor there had arranged their return and were amazed at the difficulties which had so long delayed our departure from Czernigov. Though the road we had taken from Brobruisk was no turnpike but a country road, we made good time along it nevertheless. We passed the sizeable town of Sluck, the smaller one of Romanev-Nieszewiecz, which still bore the traces of the sharp engagement there between the Russians and the Austrians in 1812,* the towns of Slonim, Sabelin and Grodek, and on 16th February arrived at Bialystok, having covered, from Bobruisk, a distance of 215 miles in 13 days. Almost everywhere, with very few exceptions, we had found a friendly reception, though nowhere were we fed free of charge. The weather was cold but not extreme and the sleighing generally good. The landscape throughout was nordic in character. Some districts were densely wooded, others so treeless that the inhabitants had to use straw for fuel. Nowhere did it present the varied aspect to which we are accustomed in Germany, being almost uniformly monotonous. Even the valleys marking the courses of brooks and rivers all looked alike and, to put it bluntly, dreary.

In Bialystok, to our great delight, we met Major von Seybothen, a Württemberg officer charged with the duty of receiving Württembergers returning from Russia, and with him Commissary Ruoff, who had authority to provide them with funds. Only now were we able to regard ourselves as free men. With a month's salary which we received in advance, and money which

---

* The Austrians, under Count von Schwartzenberg, played a rather passive role on Napoleon's right flank during the Russian campaign. They failed to prevent Admiral Chichagov from taking Minsk and joining forces with the main Russian army to challenge, however ineptly, Napoleon's crossing of the Berezina.

we borrowed from Ruoff, we bought the most necessary clothing, and what was left went on some of the comforts of which we had been starved for so long, such as a good meal and a decent bottle of wine. Here also I was given medicine by Surgeon Pommer, the regimental medical officer, which at last delivered me completely and permanently from my persistent diarrhoea. Major von Seybothen told me that he was particularly charged by the King to obtain news of me because rumours had reached Württemberg that I had taken service with the Russians' German legion. He was happy to see these rumours scotched by my arrival, which he would report to Stuttgart immediately. He also informed me that after my capture I had been transferred to the 5th Cavalry Regiment.

We stayed eight days in Bialystok, recuperating a little from our hardships, but the time was too short to afford us more than a modest reserve of strength with which to face those that still lay ahead. The city is pleasantly situated and has some fine buildings dating from its Prussian days. The taverns are passable and we frequented them more assiduously, of course, than any other part of the town.

Major von Seybothen gave us detailed instructions for our journey back to Ludwigsburg. We were to travel with relay horses either by sleigh or coach and were to have free quarters and board at every staging post—an arrangement welcomed by soldiers even in normal times and by us the more so since, with the modest funds at our disposal, we would otherwise have had to go begging most of the way. Days of rest were now not even mentioned. On the contrary, it was the wish of the King that we should return as speedily as possible. This order coincided with our own dearest wishes, and it was certainly not our fault if every now and again we had to spend more than one night in the same place. It was predictable, however, that until we reached the German frontier our journey would be fraught with occasional delays owing to disobliging Russian officials who placed obstacles in our way, and to the understandable ill will of the inhabitants of the Duchy of Warsaw who would now regard us, the allies of Russia, as their enemies. Our prescribed route lay largely through country already familiar to me from my travels as a prisoner of war or during the campaign of 1812, so I will refrain from repeating what is already known and confine myself to the description of incidents along the way which may be of general interest.

In Bialystok we were joined by Colonel von Seeger and Captain von Sonntag, and with the former in command of our party we left the city on 24th February in the direction of Plonsk, reaching Tykocyn, the first town in the Duchy of Warsaw, by nightfall. During the next four days we travelled by way of Lomza, Ostrolenka and Pultusk, reaching Plonsk on the 28th without encountering any adventures of note. Here we had to put in a day of rest for lack of horses, and crossed the Vistula on 2nd March in the direction of Gabin. On this stretch of road Butsch and I lost contact with our companions, falling behind with a poor team of horses and our driver losing his way. Only by covering two stages with special teams at breakneck speed were we able to catch up with them again at Kalisch on the 3rd. This mishap led to another. For when we entered the gates of Kalisch we were stopped by the officer on guard who took us without further ado for escaped French prisoners of war. We were hustled off to the guardroom and grossly insulted. After much argument they finally took us under escort to the town commandant who released us after a brief interrogation. As a result of this unpleasant incident we were too late to find a billet and had to put up at an inn. Fortunately we happened to choose the Hotel de Pologne whose owner, Herr Woelfel, a Stuttgarter by birth, not only made us very welcome but also remembered that we were his countrymen when he presented us with the bill. Next day we found a billet with a nice man called Meyer where, for the first time for months, I had the pleasure of sleeping in a proper bed again. Before our departure on 5th March Herr Woelfel treated us all to spiced punch and a selection of other acceptable drinks. Beyond Ostrow, the same misfortune as Captain Butsch and I had experienced befell the entire party: we lost our way and blundered into a village occupied by Russian infantry who gained the same mistaken impression as the officer on guard at the gates of Kalisch. As it proved impossible to convince these people of their error—and this the less since Colonel von Seeger treated them very arrogantly—we were finally dragged under escort and with much abuse and bad language to Przygoczkij, a fine estate belonging to Prince Radziewill, where a senior officer was in residence. But there we all but jumped out of the frying pan into the fire. This Russian officer, on hearing what had occurred, fiercely resented the blows with the flat of his sword which Colonel Seegers had so liberally dispensed among his men and threatened to pack us off back to Kalisch in irons. Our leader replying in equally unmeasured terms it was some time before peace was restored between us. We then learned that the soldiers would have been quite content to let us continue on our way on payment of a small bounty. Now, however, their fury against us had risen to a pitch which made us fear the worst and forced the Russian commander to order a parade of his men for the following morning, to enable us to slip away unobserved while it was in progress till we were out of reach of the maddened soldiery. The rest of the

L

evening we spent amicably in the company of the Russian officers at their hospitable table, and slept the night in the manor house. Next day we reached the Silesian frontier.

On our journey from Bialystok to the Silesian frontier we had fared much as we had anticipated. The Russian commandants in Poland showed no greater urge to speed us on our way than had their colleagues in Russia. Some had never heard of Württemberg, others had no idea where to find it on the map, but all were of the opinion that it must be a very small country since they knew so little about it. They therefore concluded that Russia could attach but little weight to her alliance with so puny a power, and that they for their part were unlikely to incur much blame if they took scant notice of our demands for a rapid passage. They were also quick to remind us that we had initially opposed them, joining them only when Fortune smiled upon their arms. The Polish authorities, expectably, showed themselves even more indifferent. They could hardly be blamed for hampering our progress at every turn, knowing as they did that we were on our way to swell the ranks of their enemies. Among the inhabitants there was a universal air of gloom at the misfortunes that had befallen the French armies, and the very same people who had treated us with kindness when we came as prisoners now showed us their indifference or even active dislike, and supplied our needs as grudgingly and inadequately as possible. But it must be remembered that the duchy had suffered terribly from the war and, poor as it had been before, was now literally beggared. Not even the Jews with all their thrift and ingenuity could make ends meet any longer as well as paying the heavy taxes and war levies imposed on them. Like everyone else they yearned for easement of their burdens, but in contrast to the Poles did not expect it from the French whom they had ruthlessly exploited and whose vengeance they feared as a result.

We were glad to shake the dust of unhappy Poland from our feet and to step on German soil once more. The day we left the Duchy of Warsaw we crossed the Oder at Steinau and made haste to pass through Silesia where, despite our lately concluded alliance, we could not expect a very warm welcome. Indeed, it could hardly have been otherwise as during the armistice of 1813 the Württemberg army corps had been stationed in Silesia* and, despite every possible consideration, had incurred the profound dislike of the country's freedom-loving inhabitants. But to the Silesians' credit I must emphasize that their behaviour, though aloof, was never churlish and that they refrained from any kind of insult. Their occasional suggestion that the South Germans would have done better to join Prussia and the rest of Germany earlier in 1813 was one with which we could not but agree.

My first action on German soil was to inform my mother, who had not heard a word from me since I was taken prisoner, that I was alive and well. This I did on 7th March in the small town of Lübben. Travelling via Haynau, Bunzlau and Naumburg we reached Saxony on the 10th.

Our first night on Saxon soil was spent at Görlitz and next day we passed through the bustling and prosperous town of Bautzen, reaching Dresden on the 12th. From Lauben onward the ravages of the war of 1813 were much in evidence. Every-

* Fearful of over-extending his lines of communication in potentially hostile country, Napoleon negotiated an armistice with Russia and Prussia from the beginning of July to the middle of August 1813. The French and their allies—Württemberg still among them—occupied Saxony, Silesia and parts of Bohemia.

where there were gutted houses, hamlets and even whole villages. Every now and again we could see a new building rising from the ashes. Bautzen itself had suffered severely from the battle of 21st May 1813 and displayed the ruins of a great conflagration. The town of Bischoffswerda, which was completely destroyed during the battle, still lay in ruins. The inhabitants were depressed and discouraged. Their country had been a battlefield and their homes and fields cruelly ravaged for so long that their spirit had been broken perhaps for years to come. And yet the burdens of foraging armies crossing their land and settling on their homes like locusts still continued. The good Lusatians' only comfort in all this was the hope that, industrious and well-governed as they are and with their soil so rich and bountiful, they would recover more quickly from the scourge of war than many another district equally ravaged but less blessed. As far as we personally were concerned the Lusatians treated us very decently and invariably went farther out of their way to meet our modest demands than either duty demanded or we could reasonably expect.

In the afternoon of 12th March we took the romantic road from Stolpen to Dresden, entering the city by the fine stone bridge over the Elbe. All the fortifications which the French had built here in 1813 remained intact and seemed in fine condition. The residence of the King of Saxony had been transformed into a proper and quite formidable fortress. The garrison consisted of between twelve and fifteen thousand Russians billeted on the populace whose hardships they greatly increased, both by their behaviour and by their exorbitant requisitions. The spans of the Elbe bridge that had been destroyed had now been partially repaired by means of wooden struts. The beautiful Frauenkirche had been turned into a store-house. The King had not returned to his residence after the battle of Leipzig and was being held prisoner.* The Russian governor, Prince Repnin, administered the country in his stead. The people were visibly despondent and gloomy and we deeply sympathized with their afflictions. Had we been able to avoid it, and had our funds permitted, we would certainly have refrained both here and in Lusatia from adding to their burdens by making use of their homes as billets. In Dresden I paid at least part of the cost of my quarters, my host being a threadbare chancery clerk richly blessed with progeny.

There was nothing to keep us in Dresden longer than absolutely necessary and we continued our journey at noon next day in a south-westerly direction.

Since our departure from Bialystok one of us had always travelled ahead to arrange accommodation and new horses for the rest of the party. Since this was a most difficult and unpleasant assignment there were no volunteers for it, and all of us had to take turns. It was now my turn and remained so through Chemnitz, Zwickau and Plauen in Saxony, and Hof, Münchberg and Bayreuth in Bavaria, where we arrived after three days' travel on 10th March. Though the Erz mountain range and the Voigtland presented a less desolate spectacle than those parts of Saxony through which our journey had hitherto taken us, the disastrous war had left its traces here as well. But what hurt these provinces even more than the war itself was the damage it

* King Frederick Augustus of Saxony changed his allegiance from Prussia to France after the battle of Jena in 1806 and was rewarded by Napoleon with the Grand Duchy of Warsaw. But though he personally kept faith with the French from then on, this policy was not popular with his subjects. At the battle of Leipzig the Saxon contingent deserted to the Allies and the King was taken prisoner. At the subsequent peace settlement Saxony lost a great deal of territory but Frederick Augustus was allowed to remain on the throne.

had done to trade, commerce and industry, depriving innumerable merchants, artisans and workers of their livelihood for months on end. We hurried on to escape these scenes of misery, staying nowhere longer than necessary and ever at pains to make the fewest possible demands on our hosts, contenting ourselves with what the people, out of their generosity and poverty, were prepared and able to provide without asking.

On entering Bavaria the scene was transformed. Here the war had never penetrated to destroy the country's wealth. The people had heard its rumblings only from afar, though they had, of course, suffered from it indirectly in the shape of higher taxes. But their homesteads at least were spared, and their sacrifices imposed for the sake of the country's welfare could be made good by a little added industry and thrift. Our fare became ampler, and despite the hardships we had suffered on the journey we felt our strength gradually returning.

We had our first Bavarian billet in Hof, and on the 16th travelled by way of Münchberg to Bayreuth, which is a considerable city. Thus far we had travelled by sleigh all the way from Czernigov. But now the thaw set in and spring burst forth rapidly and gaily. Our spirits rose, the ice that had paralysed our feelings for so long also began to melt, indifference and stupor gave way to merriment and joy in good company. Gradually we found ourselves able to contemplate with calm minds our return home and the welcome in store for us from our loved ones.

For some time before leaving Czernigov I had been suffering from an open wound on my left foot. The strenuous journey had not only made it worse but caused a similar sore to appear on my other foot. In Bayreuth, therefore, I was excused further service as quartermaster. My place was taken by Captain von Br . . ., who, however, found the task too onerous and proceeded, with our passports and relay permits in his pocket, from Bamberg on his own to Stuttgart, leaving us to make our way back as best we might. Annoying though his dereliction of duty was for us, the distance we still had to travel was not great, we took care to follow the fugitive's route as closely as possible and consequently were not greatly delayed.

We reached Bamberg on the 17th. It is an ancient city, but well built and busy, on the river Rednitz, over which there is a fine stone bridge within the city walls. On the 18th we travelled to Ritzingen—the direct route through Würzburg being barred by the French, who still held the fortress of Marienburg—and on the 19th travelled down the glorious Main valley to Ochsenfurth where we turned left towards Mergentheim.

Throughout Bavaria our reception had been all that we could expect or desire, and the people a great deal friendlier than they had been in Northern Germany.

We reached Mergentheim on the evening of the 19th. Our joy at reaching home safely was indescribable. The authorities took excellent care of us but plied us closely with enquiries about our experiences. We gladly obliged by telling them all we knew, and all that evening, until late into the night, were also surrounded at the taverns where we were lodged by crowds of attentive listeners. The town commandant had instructions to send us on to Ludwigsburg, so we travelled next day through Künzelsau to Öhringen. Here an acquaintance brought me the glad news that I had been awarded the Knight's Cross of the Military Order of Merit.*

* In striking contrast with Vossler's somewhat unspectacular promotion after the Russian campaign, this was a notable distinction. The award of the Knight's Cross of this Order entitled the recipient to place the ennobling prefix 'von' before his name—a privilege of which Vossler availed himself.

On 21st March we reached Ludwigsburg by way of Weinsberg and Heilbronn. Through a great throng of people we drove to the market square to await the governor's orders. As we waited, someone in the crowd asked for me by name and, on hearing that I was among the returned prisoners, ran off and presently returned with my elder brother. We greeted each other with heartfelt joy and only now, having seen my brother again face to face, did I fully realize that I had truly returned home. We spent the night in Ludwigsburg and next morning continued on to Stuttgart. In our travelling clothes, dirty and ragged as we were, we presented ourselves to General von Dillen, who was as surprised and shocked at our appearance as everyone else who met us. By him we were each acquainted with our future duties. I found myself assigned to the Garde du Corps Cavalry, stationed in Ludwigsburg, given a grant of twenty louis d'or towards my uniform and equipment, and decorated with my medal. Then I went to see my relatives in Stuttgart who gave me a rapturous reception.

VIII

IN these two years—1812 and 1813—I had endured not only the dangers which are the common soldier's lot but also every rigour which an unaccustomed climate, extremes of heat and cold, hunger and thirst, a total lack of all life's normal needs and comforts, a hostile people and inhospitable land could inflict. My health, once robust, was ruined. My feet were a mass of open sores, my stomach greatly weakened, unable to absorb any but the lightest of diets. My chest ached with every sudden movement. Nor had the two campaigns proved any less ruinous for my finances. Twice I had equipped myself anew out of my own pocket, had lost more than ten horses and returned dressed in rags and encumbered with debts.*

Centuries will pass and breed many more wars. Yet the horrors of the war of 1812 and the misfortunes that befell the French army and its allies will not soon be forgotten. It may well be a hundred years or more before another such army will appear on a field of battle in all its glory.

And now I end my tale, having nothing to add except that, after an eight weeks' cure in Wildbad, my shattered health still refused to mend and that I was therefore transferred to the sick list at the end of June 1814. A few days later I handed in my resignation from the Army, which was accepted.

---

* But as an invalid officer Vossler had a right to a position in the civil service of which, it seems, he also availed himself.